INFANT BAPTISM – LIFE or DEATH?

JUDY MCKENZIE MCCLARY

Magnolia Publications

Infant Baptism – Life or Death?
Judy McKenzie McClary
Published by Magnolia Publications

This book or parts thereof may not be reproduced in any form, stored in a retrieval system, or transmitted in any form by any means —electronic, mechanical, photocopy, recording, or otherwise—without prior written permission of the publisher, except as provided by United States of America copyright law.

Unless otherwise noted, all Scripture quotations are from the New King James Version. Copyright © 1982 by Thomas Nelson, Inc. Used by permission. All rights reserved.

Scripture quotations marked AMP are from the Amplified Bible. Old Testament copyright © 1965, 1987 by the Zondervan Corporation. The Amplified New Testament copyright © 1954, 1958, 1987 by the Lockman Foundation. Used by permission.

Scripture quotations marked NIV are from the Holy Bible, New International Version of the Bible. Copyright © 1973, 1978, 1984, International Bible Society. Used by permission.

Scripture quotations marked NLT are taken from the Holy Bible, New Living Translation, copyright © 1996, 2004, 2007 by Tyndale House Foundation. Used by permission of Tyndale House Publishers, Inc., Carol Stream, Illinois 60188. All rights reserved.

Scripture quotations marked KJV are from The Holy Bible, Old and New Testaments in the King James Version.

Previous Title: *The Secret About Infant Baptism That Everyone's Missing;* published by *Creation House, Lake Mary, FL.*
ISBN: 978-1-59979-170-8
Library of Congress Control Number: 2007924894

Revised and expanded
Copyright © 2008–2018 Judy McKenzie McClary
All rights reserved
ISBN 978-1-93938-712-7
Printed in the United States of America
Available at amazon.com and other retail outlets

This book is lovingly dedicated to my husband, Charles, who has consistently given me support and encouragement as I researched and wrote on the essential issue of baptism and the Church.

CONTENTS

Introduction 1

Part I: Does Baptism Save?

1. Too Many Baptisms 7
2. Doctrinal Diversity 15
3. Called to Write 21
4. Back to School 35
5. The Answer Cometh 41
6. Seven Letters Sent 45
7. Ancient Heresy Uncovered 49
8. Luther's Flip-Flop 59
9. Noah, the Goddess Religions & Infant Baptism . 69

Part II: Infant Baptism Corrupts the Church

10. Purple Scarlet Harlot 89
11. Rome's Certificate 97
12. Killing Christians Over Infant Baptism 101
13. Baptism & the Spanish Inquisition 111
14. The Reformation Revisited 117
15. The Luther Nobody Knows 133
16. Birds of a Feather 145
17. Ancient Church in the Alps 157
18. Inquisition Enters Colonial Shores 171
19. Separation of Church & State 177

Appendix I 10 Myths of Infant Baptism 185
Appendix II Back to Faith Alone 193
Author's Page 199
Author's Books 201
Bibliography 203

INTRODUCTION

God is moving mysteriously in these last days regarding the subject of water baptism. Never before has He been so determined to bring truth to the forefront. The worldwide Church has two branches, two modes of water baptism, and teaches two wildly different ways of getting to heaven—with one branch believing that baptism saves infants and the other believing it does not.

This confusion can be seen in a book on the subject written by a recently retired Lutheran pastor. His book attributes the many spiritual benefits of water baptism to infant baptism. He closes his book by saying that, although a baptism of infants "can't be proved or disproved," (it is not found in the Bible), he believes in it anyway.

Another strange-but-true story happened at the same church. The current pastor stood before his congregation one Sunday morning and related the following incident. He said the Lord told him to read the book of Ezekiel. He proceeded to obey, although he did not know the reason he was to do this. When he opened his Bible to Ezekiel, however, it started to shake. He said he quickly closed it.

He said he was on a plane a short time later flying somewhere when he decided to try reading

Ezekiel again. This time when he opened it, not only did his Bible begin to vibrate, so did the plane and everything in it. The pilot's shaky voice came over the intercom saying he did not know why the plane was shaking; everything pointed to good flying weather.

Remembering what had happened before, the pastor said he quickly closed his Bible and the shaking stopped. He stood before his congregation that Sunday morning asking for thirty volunteers to fast and pray for him while he tried again to read it.

That he had been asked to read the book of Ezekiel seemed mysterious to him at the time, however, it was not at all mysterious to me. My husband and I had been members of that same congregation a few years before. It was while I was writing a 12-week adult Christian education curriculum on the Holy Spirit. I was including material on Jesus' water baptism and I was poised to add material on the infant baptism practiced in our Lutheran church.

It was at that time that God stopped me and told me to read the Old Testament book of Ezekiel. In the book of Ezekiel, the story is told of God removing His presence from the Jerusalem Temple because of their idolatry.

By asking the pastor to read Ezekiel, I believe God was trying to get his attention so He could deliver a word of warning through him to the mainline denominational churches that practice an infant baptism and the belief that 'baptism saves.' 'Baptism saves' comes out of sun worship which was the same religion that the Israelites were involved in at the time when God's presence was removed from the Temple.

The first warning went out to this same church in the nineties in the form of seven letters that I researched and wrote as I uncovered the origins of infant baptism. At that time the warning was ignored even though the accuracy of the research I performed was confirmed in a front-page article in the Minneapolis *Star Tribune* within a month after the last letter was given to the pastors and elders of that church.

The article reported that a "RE-imagining" Conference would be held the next day, November 4, 1993, at the Minneapolis Convention Center. At the conference, prayer was made—not to Jesus Christ as one might expect at a conference sponsored by Christian churches—but to a mystery religions' goddess named Sophia! [1]

Uppermost in my mind was the Scripture that says a good tree cannot bear bad fruit. As I began my research into early Church history, I wanted to find out why Martin Luther put "baptism saves" into the *Augsburg Confession* rather than the statement he is so famous for—that of salvation by faith alone. I would discover conflicting interests involved in his decision and a return to an ancient heresy the apostle Paul warned would

---

[1] *Star Tribune: "The divine redefined" by Martha Sawyer Allen, staff writer, 1 Bw. 11-3-93.*

enter the Church after his demise.

There are some who will question the right of a layperson to address the salvation practices of large and important denominations. And, while it is true that I am neither a minister nor a priest, I have to ask the more educated clergy of the infant baptism denominations the inevitable question—Why hasn't the controversy over infant baptism been made public from the pulpit?

Why was it left for a little-known (but very curious) layperson to find out and make public? My best guess is that you didn't know either!

Clergy and laypeople alike—*we have all been duped. We need to join hands, repent, and get back on track.*

PART I

DOES BAPTISM SAVE?

Then Peter said to them, "Repent, and let every one of you be baptized in the name of Jesus Christ for the remission of sins; and you shall receive the gift of the Holy Spirit.

—Acts 2:38

1

Too Many Baptisms

When I was growing up as a little girl in a Presbyterian church, I was very much aware that not all churches believed alike. My cousin, Mary, was Roman Catholic, but I would never have asked her straight out why her church taught about purgatory when ours did not.

There was another church nearby that the family of one of my sister's friends attended. Without it ever being openly discussed, I knew that church had less status than our Presbyterian church, but even though I sensed some churches were more socially accepted than others, I did not understand why.

Another thing that was never discussed in polite circles was the fact that some churches had a different baptism than ours. Again, I did not know why. As I got older and my interest in theological matters grew, I found this difference was contrary to the Bible's claim that there is only one baptism.[1]

---

[1] Ephesians 4:4–6.

I marveled at this. How could the Church so openly practice two different baptisms when the Bible says there is only one? Yet both branches seemed to believe so strongly that their baptism was the correct one. I wondered why they were not more concerned about the lack of unity this brought to the body of Christ. For if one examines the doctrines of various denominations as I have had the opportunity to do, water baptism is the main issue that separates them.

I also wondered why the two branches teach two such very different ways of getting to heaven. Why didn't the churches just get together and study Scripture as a team, as a unit, as friends and associates? That way, when they found out which baptism was the right one, they could all practice the same mode and attach the same meaning. Then the whole Church could be in unity.

When I began my search for the truth about water baptism, I had been a member of an infant baptism church for more than forty years. I officially joined (or I should say, my parents joined me) to the Presbyterian Church when I was just six weeks old. I don't remember it, of course, but my mother assured me it was so. Despite being over eighty, she clearly remembered that day, because when I was born she and my father could not agree on a name for me. So, it was not until the day of my baptism that I received my official name.

Usually in a Presbyterian church, the ritual of

infant baptism would be conducted during a church service. However, because my parents already had four other lively little ones, it was mutually agreed to celebrate my baptism at home. The next Sunday afternoon, the Presbyterian minister and his wife came out to the farm for a fried chicken dinner and to perform the baptismal ceremony. My Uncle Jim and Aunt Sadie were invited, too. They were to "stand in" for me. Mother explained this was because I was too young to have faith for my own salvation, so they became my godparents.

With dinner finished and the dishes done, my mother took me into the back bedroom to put me into my baptismal finery. She was just finishing when my father came in. He wanted to see if we were ready and to tell her that she could name me Judy if she wished. (He had wanted to name me Sally.) Together they brought me out where the guests were and announced my name would be Judith Ann.

The three of us stood before the minister as he took out the book of rituals he carried with him for just such occasions. He opened to an infant baptism ritual and read it out loud. Then, dipping his finger into a little bowl of water, he sprinkled water on my head, no doubt adding the requisite words, "In the name of the Father and the Son and the Holy Spirit."

Another job well done! The minister probably shook hands with my parents, said good-by to the guests, chucked me under the chin, and left for home rejoicing that he had added one more soul to the great and glorious Church above and to the small Presbyterian church downtown.

Years later I wondered, Can baptism really do all the things that parents expect for infants on the day they are baptized? Would I indeed have gone to heaven if I had died that night? What if I had remained un-sprinkled? Would God still have taken me to heaven if I had not been baptized? And where in the Bible does it say that my baptism did all that for me?

Water baptism is an interesting subject. Wars have been fought over the mode and meaning behind it. Men have been burned at the stake or drowned in a raging river because they did not agree with the official method of water baptism practiced by the state Church of their day. Women have been put in stocks and flogged because they taught other women that there was something about water baptism as taught in their church that did not quite line up with their reading of Scripture.

Anne Hutchinson, of colonial Salem, Massachusetts, was one of these believed to be full of devils because she questioned the way the Church of England and the Puritan Church of her day taught water baptism. Though she was pregnant, she was mercilessly forced to flee with her husband and children to keep from being arrested and imprisoned for her beliefs. Miscarrying because of the tragedy,[2] it was spread about by her midwife that her undeveloped fetus was misshapen because he was the devil's offspring.

Even earlier, in 1565, the Spanish Inquisition was reaching itchy fingers into the southern part of what is now the United States. Its intent was to discipline residents in St. Augustine, Florida, who would not practice Church doctrine the way the official state Church of Europe wanted it practiced in the new colony. Two hundred fifty-three men, women, and infants lay dead before the ten ships sent from the mother country finished their task, raised anchor, and sailed for home.[3]

There are not many books written on the subject of water baptism. In daring to examine the subject, I am aware that discussing religion—and water baptism in particular—is not done in today's world of political correctness. Nevertheless, reopen the subject I must, for the salvation of millions (and their eternal destination) is at stake.

Now is the time that the truth about infant baptism must become clear, for it is primarily the teaching of two modes of water baptism and the value assigned to each that has kept the Church separated for centuries.

Studying the subject of water baptism is im-

---

[2] http://lcweb2.loc.go/ammem/today/jul20.html#hutchinson; http://loc.go/exhibits/religion/relo1-2.htm, accessed February 18, 2006.
[3] Harold J. Chadwick, ed., *Foxe's Book of Martyrs: Updated to the 21st Century* (Gainesville, FL: Bridge-Logos, 2001), 285–287.

portant, for the Bible says there are six principles of Christianity that we must understand if we are to mature as Christians. Note that the doctrine of baptisms is listed right alongside such important doctrines as eternal judgment and resurrection of the dead.

> "Therefore, leaving the discussion of the elementary principles of Christ, let us go on to perfection, not laying again the foundation of repentance from dead works and of faith toward God, *of the doctrine of baptisms*, of laying on of hands, of resurrection of the dead, and of eternal judgment."
> (Hebrews 6:1–2, emphasis added)

Discovering and teaching the one, true baptism will unify the Church that Jesus Christ left here on Earth. This is very important because Jesus' last earthly prayer on the night before He was crucified was for unity in the Church. He asked the Father for unity in the Church so that all could discover that God loves them and desires reconciliation with them. He wanted them to know of God's love so that they could all believe and be brought into the safety of His fold.[4]

Today, we are alive at an exciting time in history. Surely Jesus is returning soon. The time is now for the Father to grant the dying request of His only Son! Unity will come as denominations restudy baptism and change their church doc-

---

[4] John 17

trines to agree with the Bible.

Fractures will heal as the whole Church acknowledges and teaches the one baptism of Scripture.

2

DOCTRINAL DIVERSITY

The problem caused by having two different water baptisms is bigger than most Christians are willing to admit, if the inquiries on the World Wide Web are any indication. There were 371,000 Web sites with references to baptism in 2001.

A more recent check showed the number had grown to nearly thirty million. Today's numbers tell the story. People are longing to know the truth about water baptism. They want to know—were they saved or not—when they were baptized as infants? And is infant baptism *necessary* for salvation? They are sensing something is not quite right with the doctrine they have been told will give them eternal salvation.

Some time ago, I was having lunch with a member of our prayer group when a waitress literally stole some papers out from under my nose because they had *baptism* written across the top. We had gotten together to look over and discuss the material in the manuscript, and I had laid it aside for just a moment while we prepared to order.

As we studied the menus, a waitress approached our table. When she completed writing down our selections, the young lady, barely out of her teens, picked up the menus and then seemed to hesitate just a moment as she glanced over at my manuscript. She thanked us for our orders, set the menus down on my papers, and suddenly swooped everything up and headed for the kitchen.

It all happened so fast. It was my only copy! Summoning another waitress, I quickly told her what had happened and she took off for the kitchen on the run to retrieve the papers.

It wasn't long before the first girl reappeared, papers in hand, tears running down her cheeks. I tried to set her at ease. I told her I didn't think she meant any harm. I even said I didn't think she planned on keeping the manuscript. But she only cried harder, pausing just long enough to blurt out, "Oh, but I did take them on purpose!" And then she told me the following: "It seems I just don't know right from wrong anymore. I was living with my boyfriend and we got pregnant. We want to do what's right for the baby and all and get back into church, but we aren't sure which is the right church anymore."

She said she had been raised Catholic but her boyfriend didn't like attending church anymore. She had taken my papers because she wanted to "find out stuff for the baby." And then she started to cry again.

Seeing her so troubled and because of the

events she had related to me, I asked her, "Are you worried about whether God will forgive you?" I thought I could show her in the Bible what God says about forgiveness, and maybe that would relieve her mind.

But she answered no. "I'm not worried about that," she said, "because my grandma is Pentecostal and she explained salvation to me already. But now she says the Bible also says to be baptized in water to show Jesus that I really meant what I prayed."

The girl went on to explain that she had asked the priest from her church to baptize her, but he had turned her down, saying she had been baptized when she was a baby and that was enough for her. "I just don't know what's right anymore," she said, beginning to cry again.

I have not been able to forget how disturbed that young waitress was about what part water baptism should play in being right with God. She had tried to seek out answers from two people she trusted, but she only came away with more confusion because each gave her a different answer.

Her problem with the contradicting doctrines of the two branches of the Church is not all that unusual, for strangely enough, a similar incident occurred a short time later that reminded me once again how much pain and turmoil false Church doctrine causes people as they try to know God and go to heaven when they die.

At that time, I had been visiting Orlando, Florida, spending a few days with my husband while he was on a business trip. We had to take separate flights home and his was later, so he dropped me off at the airport. I entered the plane early and settled in my seat as later passengers boarded. I pulled my Bible out of my carry-on, intending to read while I waited. It was not long before a woman in her mid-seventies entered the plane and started slowly down the aisle. As she passed each row, she carefully examined the numbers on the outside seats.

When she came to my row, she found it matched the number on her ticket, and she stowed her bag under the seat and sat down. Almost immediately, she looked across at me and started to engage me in conversation. I learned that she and her husband had been farmers in Iowa and that she was alone now and owned a small condo in Florida. She was on her way to Phoenix, where she and several of her six children were gathering for Thanksgiving the next day.

Noting my open Bible, she said she had been raised Methodist but had married a Catholic. She had taken instruction in the Catholic Church before marriage and had signed over her children to be raised in the Catholic faith. None of them had been religious as children, but now two were attending Lutheran churches, one was still Roman Catholic, two had become Mormons, and the last had become a Pentecostal.

She said this diversity was threatening to tear her family apart. "I tell them all roads lead to heaven," she said. "I tell them don't talk about religion, but my Pentecostal son says all roads do not lead to heaven. He tells his brothers and sisters they aren't even going to get there unless they find out what the Bible says about salvation." She sighed, "It's getting so I hate to even go to family gatherings anymore."

I asked her what she believed, and she pondered my question before answering. "To tell you the truth," she finally said, "I don't know. But I'm getting old—*and I need to know!*"

3

CALLED TO WRITE

My research into the subject of infant baptism began when a staff member at our five thousand-member Lutheran church asked me to write a twelve-week Bible course for their adult Christian education department. They wanted a class that would study the Holy Spirit and the gifts He brings to the body of Christ. I was asked to help develop the new curriculum because I had written Bible studies before.

At first, I had not been sure whether I wanted to do this. While I found the subject of the Holy Spirit fascinating and had always thought that someday I would like to write a full-length book on the third person of the Trinity, I knew writing on the Holy Spirit would open up the subject of water baptism. I wasn't sure that was a good idea in the Lutheran church we were then attending.

After all those years, I was being confronted with the issue that had caused me so many questions. It did not seem that I could possibly write curriculum on the Holy Spirit and skirt the subject of water baptism. After all, it was the Holy Spirit who empowered Jesus to do His mighty miracles and it happened at the time of His water baptism.

Because of the part played by the Holy Spirit in the baptismal waters of the River Jordan, the subject would definitely need to be addressed. The students would ask questions about what actually happened to Jesus in water baptism and whether He was immersed or sprinkled. And was something supposed to happen inside of believers today like what happened inside of Jesus on that day? I was concerned because the topic of water baptism is volatile in the Christian Church.

I thought about the story of Jesus' water baptism. John the Baptist had at first refused to baptize Him because He sensed that Jesus was no ordinary man. He somehow knew Jesus had no sin of which He needed to repent, and John's baptism was a baptism of repentance. God had sent him to offer to the citizens of Israel a baptism for the remission of sin.

But why, John wondered, would Jesus want to take part in such a water baptism when He was without sin? Jesus stood firm. He told John it was *necessary* for Him to do this so He could "fulfill all righteousness." John still did not understand, but he agreed to baptize Jesus after telling Him that it was *he* who needed to be baptized by *Him!*[1]

There are only a very few things about Christ's

---

[1] Matthew 3:13–15

life that appear in all four Gospels, but John's baptism of repentance is one of them. All four writers shout the fact that Jesus came for the very purpose of baptizing believers with—believe it or not—the Holy Spirit![2] It was to be the major event, so I knew it must have been a very important event to God the Father and God the Holy Spirit.

So, I decided it must be important enough to me, too, that I would boldly examine it in the curriculum I was writing. I said yes to developing the curriculum, and having made that decision, I spent a year doing research before I began writing. My goal was to show that the Holy Spirit was equally active throughout both the Old Testament and the New Testament.

I wanted to show this to students through incidents taken directly from the Bible. That way, they would understand that they could embrace the Holy Spirit and not think He was some strange and recent idea thought up by man's imagination. I wanted them to welcome the Holy Spirit's ministry to and through them.

After all, God had sent His Holy Spirit to believers as a helper and a friend, according to the New Testament book of John.[3] I would show them, using His own words, how important Jesus considered the Holy Spirit to be as He explained the benefits of the Holy Spirit to His disciples.

---

[2] Matthew 3:11
[3] John 14:16

> "Nevertheless, I tell you the truth. It is to your advantage that I go away; for if I do not go away, the Helper will not come to you; but if I depart, I will send Him to you."
>
> (John 16:7)

In *The Amplified Bible,* it is more descriptive—more like we would understand if we were familiar with the depths of the Greek language. Thus, in Jesus' explanation of the "Helper" and the benefits He brings to the body of Christ, there is more explanation of the benefits Jesus experienced in His own life by being indwelt and led by the Holy Spirit.

> "However, I am telling you nothing but the truth when I say it is profitable (good, expedient, advantageous) for you that I go away. Because if I do not go away, the Comforter (Counselor, Helper, Advocate, Intercessor, Strengthener, Standby) will not come to you [into close fellowship with you]; but if I go away, I will send Him to you [to be in close fellowship with you]."
>
> (John16:7 AMP)

Soon I finished my research and was ready to write one session a week. My husband and I would then, on weekends, use a team-teaching approach to present this material to a pilot class of twelve. Doing it was great fun, and the group was unusually enthusiastic. We got instant feedback; the students insisted they had never grown so fast spiritually.

But this euphoria would soon come to an end; and, of course, the trouble started the week I began writing about water baptism. I looked up the word *baptism* in my *Strong's Exhaustive Concordance of Bible Words*, which lists every word in the Bible and the verses in which they are included. There I found more than a hundred verses referring to baptisms so I gave that week's curriculum the title *Baptisms! Baptisms! Baptisms!*

As I pondered this development, I looked each up in my Bible, I saw they referred to six different baptisms; more if one considered household baptisms (the same Acts 2:38 baptism but of multiple family members) or baptizing the dead (so-named because those publicly baptized often literally took their lives in their hands.[4] A contemporary example might be seen in the Middle East today when a Muslim converts to Christianity and is publicly baptized, often resulting in his death).

Analyzing the situation, I soon realized the six baptisms fell into a neat pattern of three old covenant and three new covenant baptisms.[5] The first two of the old covenant baptisms were Noah's baptism, when the floodwaters covered over and drowned Noah's enemies while he and his family continued on in safety in the ark;[6] and Moses' baptism, in which the waters of the Red

---

[4] *The Hebrew-Greek Key Word Bible*, P. 1696; *A Dictionary of the Bible*, pp. 74-75; *Funk & Wagnalls New Standard Bible Dictionary*, 94.
[5] Acts 2:38
[6] 1 Peter 3:20–21

Sea covered over and drowned the enemies of the children of Israel while they continued on in safety.[7]

The third old covenant baptism was John's baptism of repentance for the remission of sin.[8] Technically, John's baptism was a bridge between the ending of the old covenant and the beginning of the new covenant. Though written about in the New Testament, it is still an old covenant baptism because Jesus had not yet shed His blood, which would ratify the new and better covenant. I set those baptisms aside as not being immediately relevant to the new covenant believer.

There were also three new covenant baptisms. In the following two verses, water baptism for the remission of sins is explained in the Acts Scripture; and in the Luke Scripture, it is taught that Jesus will baptize with the Holy Spirit and with fire.

> "...Repent, and let every one of you be baptized in the name of Jesus Christ for the remission of sins; and you shall receive the gift of the Holy Spirit."
>
> (Acts 2:38)

> "I indeed baptize you with water; but One mightier than I is coming, whose sandal strap I am not worthy to loose. He will baptize you with the Holy Spirit and fire."
>
> (Luke 3:16)

---

[7] 1 Corinthians 10:1–2
[8] Matthew 3:1–11

The three baptisms mentioned in the above two verses were (1) an after-conversion water baptism, (2) the Holy Spirit baptism, and (3) a baptism of fire—the last two being irretrievably linked together for when one receives the Holy Spirit, they must be prepared for both extraordinary joy and fiery trials.

It is interesting that both John's baptism and Jesus' baptism have similar wording; both are for the "remission of sins." In both baptisms, although Jesus' blood had not yet been shed when John's baptism was in effect so it was under the old covenant, both still accomplished the same benefit: the *remission* of sins—which, in the Greek, means *remission, pardon, deliverance, forgiveness, and liberty.*[9]

Though I had read all the verses in the Bible that referred to baptism, there did not seem to be any biblical way to validate infant baptism. In our church, this is very serious. Members are taught from a young age that they were saved as babies when they were baptized.[10] Now I was left without any evidence about our church's baptism to complete that weekend's lesson.

I had been working late at church all that week trying to find Scripture to use to prove an infant baptism and complete the lesson. I finally had no recourse but to call our pastor at home. Surely he would have studied the subject in seminary

---

[9] Strong's Exhaustive Concordance of the Bible. 15. (Greek #859).
[10] Matthew 18:3

and could give me some answers.

When he picked up the phone that evening, I explained who I was and that I was having difficulty finding Scripture to verify infant baptism. But first, I asked whether he really believed in infant baptism. I did this respectfully, because he was the one who conducted the Sunday morning baptismal ceremonies at our church. I had noticed that although he gave the same verse every Sunday, it referred to small children but not to water baptism. It was Jesus' response to His disciples' question about which of them would be greatest in the kingdom of heaven.

True, a little child is mentioned in that verse, but in reality the disciples were asking Jesus which of them would be greatest in the Kingdom of God. But I found no mention of a baptism of infants in the Bible and now I wondered why our churches don't do a blessing instead of a baptism over infants and small children? This is something the Bible does instruct us in. Parents brought their children to Jesus so that He might pray a blessing over them (some churches call it dedicating). The disciples scolded the parents but Jesus rebuked them for their actions and prayed a blessing over the children.

The Jews are very big on such a blessing. On their Friday night Sabbaths, the head of the house starts by blessing his wife, then he individually blesses each of his children by name— moving from there to blessing anyone else who is present as a guest; then, finally he blesses the food and the drink.

Because Jesus had purposely taught in the New Testament on blessing children and infants, I wondered why our church didn't do a "blessing" over children instead of substituting a "baptism" of infants?

But the pastor assured me in no uncertain terms that he did *indeed* believe in infant baptism! In fact, he said, his assurance grew year by year, "even though infant baptism is not found in the Bible, *per se*." He said this was because it is *hidden* in Scripture. He told me to do a word search of Old Testament circumcision and I would find plenty of information to validate a baptism of infants.

He added that infant baptism was a "*thinly-veiled*" type of New Testament circumcision and that because the ritual of Old Testament circumcision "saved" under the old covenant, the ritual of infant baptism "saves" under the new covenant, because it is a thinly-veiled type of New Testament circumcision."

Then he added one more thing before hanging up. He told me that I should also look up all the New Testament passages that refer to household baptisms. "With these two things—circumcision and household baptisms," he assured me, "you will have more than enough material to finish the lesson on baptism for this weekend's class."

He hung up, and I started looking up Bible verses with the words *circumcise, circumcised*, or *circumcision* in them. As I began to read the verses, I was shocked to discover that the Bible does not teach that circumcision saves at all. In fact, it teaches that if we believe that circumcision saves, we will fall from grace.

> "Indeed, I, Paul, say to you that if you become circumcised, Christ will profit you nothing. And I testify again to every man who becomes circumcised that he is a debtor to keep the whole law. You have become estranged from Christ, you who attempt to be justified by law; you have fallen from grace."
> (Galatians 5:2–4)

I looked up even more verses containing the words *circumcise* and *circumcision* in them and discovered that, contrary to what my denomination teaches, the New Testament does not say that circumcision saves. More than one book of the Bible warns that we are not to believe the ritual of circumcision is a part of new covenant salvation.

> "For what does the Scripture say? "Abraham believed God, and it [not circumcision] was accounted to him for righteousness."
> (Romans 4:3)

And then the question is asked:

> "How then was it accounted? While he was circumcised, or uncircumcised? Not while circumcised, but while uncircumcised."
> (Romans 4:10)

As I began to study the ritual of Old Testament

circumcision, I learned that Abraham, the patriarch of our faith, was not saved by the ritual of circumcision. He was not even circumcised until twenty-five years after God called him righteous solely because of his faith.[11] His circumcision, according to God, was to be a sign of the faith he already had.[12] Therefore, I had to conclude that the information I had been given was wrong. I had to conclude that if the original circumcision of the old covenant did not save the father of our faith, then a thinly-veiled type of that circumcision—as my denomination calls infant baptism—would not save either.

Concerned, I started researching the second clue I had received, that of household baptisms. First of all, I wanted to see if Scripture said—in words—that infants were included when whole households were baptized; or if it stated that all who were baptized were first believers. I decided my criteria for whether someone was a believer would be if they listened to the gospel as it was preached and then consciously made a decision to believe based on what they had heard.

There are five examples of household baptisms in the New Testament. Because the Philippian jailer's household is most often mentioned as sterling proof that babies were included in household baptisms, I decided to start there. I began by carefully examining the following vers-

---

[11] Genesis 15:6
[12] Genesis 17:9–14

es. The key, I felt, lay in the last verse, where it clearly states that the jailer's entire household believed before they were baptized.

> "But at midnight Paul and Silas were praying and singing hymns to God, and the prisoners were listening to them. Suddenly there was a great earthquake, so that the foundations of the prison were shaken; and immediately all the doors were opened and everyone's chains were loosed. And the keeper of the prison, awaking from sleep and seeing the prison doors open, supposing the prisoners had fled, drew his sword and was about to kill himself. But Paul called with a loud voice, saying, "Do yourself no harm, for we are all here." Then he called for a light, ran in, and fell down trembling before Paul and Silas. And he brought them out and said, "Sirs, what must I do to be saved?" So they said, "Believe on the Lord Jesus Christ, and you will be saved, you and your household." Then they spoke the word of the Lord to him and to all who were in his house. And he took them the same hour of the night and washed their stripes. And immediately he and all his family were baptized. Now when he had brought them into his house, he set food before them; and he rejoiced, having believed in God with all his household."
>
> (Acts 16:25–34)

The Bible could not be more clear in the first four examples, one of which is the above-mentioned jailer's household baptism. In each example, it emphasizes that those who were baptized, first had personal faith.

> Jailer's household; all were believers before baptism.
> (See Acts 16:16–34, esp. v. 34.)
> Cornelius' household; all were first believers.
> (See Acts 10:1–48, esp. vv. 1, 44.)
> Stephanas' household; all were believers, then baptized.
> (See 1 Corinthians 16:15.)
> Crispus' household; all first believed.
> (See Acts 18:8.)

The fifth example is less clear. It is the story of Lydia, a seller of purple, and her household. The apostle Paul and his entourage went to Philippi, the main city in Macedonia. There they stayed for several days. On the Sabbath, he went down to the riverbank, where he found several devout women who habitually gathered for prayer on that day. The group included Lydia and her household.

Already believers in God, they listened when Paul taught the gospel of Christ. He evidently explained the need to take part in water baptism to prove one's faith in Christ was sincere, for Lydia and her household responded to his preaching by being baptized.

> "And on the Sabbath day we went out of the city to the riverside, where prayer was customarily made; and we sat down and spoke to the women who met there. Now a certain woman named Lydia heard us. She was a seller of purple from the city of Thyatira, who worshiped God. The Lord opened her heart to heed the things spoken by Paul. And when she and her household were baptized, she begged us, saying, "If you have

judged me to be faithful to the Lord, come to my house and stay." So she persuaded us."

(Acts 16:13–15)

These verses only state that women were present that day. They do not mention babies or men or children being present, so it would be presumptuous to assume that babies were present at Lydia and her household's riverside baptism. We know that Lydia listened and responded to the gospel, but Scripture is silent about her household. We could assume this to be true but we can't be sure. Therefore, it cannot be stated as actual fact.

However, it appears that our denomination's salvation doctrine lies in the silence of Scripture. The non-information found in the example of Lydia's household is not proof but apparently it has given infant baptism denominations the license to teach their members that they were saved when they were baptized as babies.

As for me, I was back where I started. Clearly, circumcision could not be used as proof of infant baptism, nor do household baptisms give concrete evidence for a baptism of infants. It did not seem possible that a Christian denomination would risk the eternal damnation of their members by teaching something that could not be found in the Bible. This bothered me.

I decided to take a year out of my life to attend a Lutheran Bible school affiliated with our church. I thought, "Surely a Lutheran school will study the subject of infant baptism, and I will find the answers for which I am looking."

4

BACK TO SCHOOL

I signed up for school that same fall. During the coming year, I would sit under more than twenty of the most respected Lutheran teachers and pastors in our area. The instructors were interesting and the school intense, as it studied every book in the Old and New Testaments in two years.

As the year went on, I began to notice something unusual that was happening. In most of my classes, the teachers would be teaching their assigned subjects, when suddenly they would abandon their notes and energetically exhort the students to accept infant baptism. There, for a period of just a few minutes, we would be heartily admonished to believe the Lutheran doctrine of salvation, which included infant baptism. Then, just as suddenly, the subject would be dropped and they would return to their classroom assignment.

I watched this happen time after time. I also noticed that no Bible verses were ever given to support their stand. I, too, had been unable to find even one reference to validate baby baptisms, so I would raise my hand to ask if they had chapter and verse to back up what we were being taught. I was invariably given the same two responses that our pastor had given me—Old Testament circumcision and New Testament household baptisms. They would become offended when I asked for proof.

I was very concerned about this, so one afternoon I made an appointment with the head of our school to talk to him about my concerns. He seemed anxious to meet with me, too. So after class the next day, I went to my appointment at his office. I knocked on his open door and he stood up and kindly motioned me to a chair.

I wasted no time launching into my story. I told him of my concern that the worldwide Church had two very different methods for getting to heaven, and I told him about writing the twelve-week study course for our church and being unable to validate the claims our church makes for salvation through a baptism of infants.

I mentioned Lydia's household. I told him the non-information in that passage was as close as I could come to backing up our denomination's stand on infant baptism but my concern was that if the silence of Scripture can be used as proof, then anyone could add anything they wanted to Church doctrine as long as the Bible did not specifically disallow it.

"For example," I said, "they could take the Scripture where it says that Peter, Jesus' disciple, was standing beside the fire in the high priest's courtyard the night before Jesus' crucifixion. Using the same criteria as was used to prove infant baptism, they could add to it by saying that Peter was selling pizza to the crowd by the fire as they warmed their hands."

I told him no one could contradict this new bit of information about Peter's entrepreneurial efforts if the silence of Scripture was all that was necessary to prove such a statement was true. I finished by saying, "This is how false religions get started."

The old gentleman just sat there for a long time after I finished. He didn't say anything. I began to get nervous and thought my example was too silly for him to respond. But finally he spoke up. "I, too, once questioned infant baptism," he said, "but I saw the light, so to speak." And he urged me to do the same.

And maybe I would have—just to please him—if he had not dropped the next bombshell. He then said, "I was never ordained, you know."

Well, of course I did not know that. He is respected as one of the genuine patriarchs in our church and he is the founder of our Bible school for laypeople. Everyone calls him "Reverend," and he has led numerous mission trips. I had always assumed he was ordained, but I had to admit it was not something I had thought about.

I could see that what he was telling me was hard for him, but he continued. He said that after taking all the coursework and graduating from a Lutheran seminary, the Lutheran denomination refused to ordain him because he was married to a Mennonite woman. I was dumbfounded. I knew his wife. She was a beautiful, kind, and godly Christian woman. How could it be that a man like him couldn't be ordained when he was married to someone of as high a Christian character as she?

He said that many years ago there had been some trouble between the Lutherans and the Mennonites over infant baptism. My ears perked up. He said the Mennonites even today are worried that the Lutheran and Catholic Churches will start persecuting them anew if they recognize who they are.

I tried to get more information from him, but he wouldn't say any more. I knew even what he had said was hard for him. But I was shocked. Even then, I really did not understand. The idea of one church persecuting another church was so foreign to me.

Little did I know that the time would come when I would find answers to my questions through a three-inch thick, ancient, and obscure book that I found in a little Mennonite museum in Canada. This book, *Martyrs Mirror*, lists a multitude of men, women, and children whose blood was spilled all over Europe by the Roman Catholic Church and, later, by some of the founders of Protestant churches as well; because they did not believe infant baptism was biblical, refused to baptize their own babies, and told others.

As I left the founder's office that day, I had many things to ponder, but I knew quitting my search for the truth was not one of them. In fact, I desired more than ever to find out why the Church has two branches, two baptisms and two different ways of salvation.

There was no way I could stop now.

5

THE ANSWER
COMETH

Day by day, I continued to search for answers. One day, after a particularly harsh rebuke from a visiting pastor because of my questions, I decided not to join the other students at coffee break.

Frankly, I was feeling foolish. My questions were making me unpopular with both students and staff. Even I knew I seemed divisive at times, even though, if the truth were known, I really wanted to get along just like everybody else but I needed to know the truth so I kept asking; hoping someone could give me insight or a Bible verse to explain their faith in infant baptism and the reason our church taught a different baptism than the one in the Bible.

So that day I walked toward the back of the room with a heavy heart. The threat always nagging me, of course, was that if I did not stop asking questions, I would get kicked out of school and embarrass my husband. We were friends with people on staff. The groomsman at our wedding was now one of the ruling elders on the church council. My husband and I were teachers at the church. Our daughter attended their day school.

Also, my curriculum was being used in several new classes and I didn't want to offend. To be honest; the temptation to drop the whole question about infant baptism was in the back of my mind as I paced back and forth at the back of the room. As I contemplated all the trouble I was getting into—God suddenly spoke to my heart. It wasn't audible, but it was very distinct. No one else heard it but me. But on the inside, I was clearly impressed with these words:

NEITHER BAPTISM NOR UN-BAPTISM MATTERS, BUT ADDING IT TO THE FINISHED WORK OF THE CROSS, NULLIFIES IT!

God had spoken to me! The words seemed to reverberate inside as I turned them over in my mind. True, I had been praying to Him about this for months but I hadn't expected Him to answer—at least not in a definite way.

At first, it was not clear to me what God was trying to say. What did the words, "Neither baptism nor un-baptism matters" mean? Could churches baptize any way they wanted? Were they free to baptize infants or adults, believers or the unconverted, according to their own discretion?

And I wondered how believing in water baptism could make one lose the benefits of the cross? Yet the word God had just given me said that making baptism necessary for salvation would nullify the benefits Christ had won for us on the cross.

I continued to ponder the words I had heard, and the Lord brought to my mind a Bible verse I had memorized years ago. I compared the two, noticing how very similar in meaning they were, except that the Bible verse referred to a ritual of circumcision and the word the Lord had given me had referred to a ritual of baptism.

> "Neither circumcision nor uncircumcision avails anything, but faith working through love."
> (Galatians 5:6)

I asked the Lord to help me understand and slowly I realized the seriousness of what He had just shown me. In fact, it was so serious, it almost took my breath away for I remembered a Sunday school class taught by the pastor at a church we attended. The class was entitled *Great Doctrines of the Church.* The first Sunday we joined the class, the pastor had chosen to teach about an error that had gotten into the early Church. He said contemporary historians called the error the *dreaded* Heresy of the Judaizer—it was the worst because it was the most subtle.

This error came about because some false brethren from Judea had come insisting that the apostle Paul teach that even under the new covenant, one must be circumcised in order to be saved. The apostle refused to preach this, saying that a ritual did not save and that they would fall from grace if they put their faith in a ritual.[1]

---
[1] Acts 15

The pastor, however, assured his class that the Jerusalem Council had dealt with the Heresy of the Judaizer long ago. He said it was no longer a problem for the Christian Church.

But was he wrong? Had a ritual of infant baptism merely been substituted for the ritual of circumcision?

6

SEVEN LETTERS SENT

School was almost over for that year when I made my startling discovery. One of the last courses we had that spring was a class taught by a retired missionary entitled World Missions.

The elderly man dearly loved the stories of Martin Luther and the early Lutheran Church. He described his great disappointment in not having enough class time to dig deeper into the great Protestant Reformation of the 1500s so that we could see how much Martin Luther had affected history.

He said that we, as Christians, had a responsibility to know the facts and understand the events that surrounded the great Reformation. He challenged us to set aside time to do research on the issues. He said both public and seminary libraries contain much information on those times and that it was still important even though it happened a long time ago.

This opened my eyes to the fact that there was a whole body of literature available having to do with the roots of my denomination—a place where I could go to research ancient Church history and learn how baptismal regeneration through infant baptism entered Church doctrines. Excited, I resolved to spend my whole summer, if necessary, researching the Reformation and the part Martin Luther played in it. Little did I know then that I was beginning a decade-long search.

In the beginning, I only wanted to know why Martin Luther had turned away from his pre-Reformation stand on salvation by faith alone and returned to the Roman Catholic belief in infant baptism (baptismal regeneration). But as time went on, I saw that the integrity of our Church was at stake.

During this time, the leadership at our church was pondering whether or not to remain under the covering of the ELCA. The denomination had just released a controversial position paper on human sexuality that had many churches belonging to that organization in an uproar.

This was not the first time they had taken nonbiblical stands about Church issues, and for this reason, our church was seeking God to see if they should remain under the covering of the ELCA as a light and a conscience or if they should get out. To help in making this decision, the pastor invited input from the congregation.

Because of the Bible verse that says a good tree cannot bear bad fruit and a bad tree cannot bear good fruit, I had begun to wonder what it was in the roots of the Lutheran Church that was causing such bad fruit to emanate from ELCA leadership. Little did I know then that by searching for these roots I would also be led to the answers on infant baptism for which I was seeking.

By going to several different libraries, I was able to find the facts summarized in these chapters. A Baptist seminary and a Lutheran seminary both provided information. The University of Minnesota library and a secular public research library were also used. My greatest find, though, came from an opportunity I had to do research in the library of a college on the East Coast whose library houses one of the finest collections in the world of early Christian documents and books.

As my research progressed, I wrote letters to my church telling them of the things I was uncovering as I searched for the roots of our denomination. With each letter I would think I had uncovered enough, but then I would find one more startling revelation and end up writing one more letter and sending it off.

At first, these letters were only for the eyes of our pastors and church council members, but as time has passed, I have come to realize that this information is even more relevant for the body of Christ today than when the letters were written a few short years ago. I have been able to uncover many things long hidden because of the prayer and fasting of our church and because of the faithful weekly prayer group that gathered together and prayed for me during this time of research. Things hidden for generations in secular and seminary libraries were uncovered.

It was during this time that I discovered more about an ancient heresy that almost destroyed the Christian church.

7

ANCIENT HERESY UNCOVERED

One of the first things I uncovered as I began my research was that, at the time when the New Testament was just being written, false teaching was already trying to enter the Church. One error in particular was so devastating that even today half the world's churches have been duped by it. Theologians call it the dreaded Heresy of the Judaizer.

The pastor at our previous church had taught on the subject of the Heresy of the Judaizer, but it took reading and rereading the book of Galatians many times at the prompting of the Lord before I saw the connection between my church's infant baptism ritual and the Old Testament ritual of circumcision. I saw that because our denomination teaches that the ritual of infant baptism is a "thinly-veiled" type of the ritual of Old Testament circumcision, the concern about the Heresy of the Judaizer also applies to our church as well as other infant baptism denominations.

The apostle Paul had warned that men who were members of the Church would bring in a devastating error: "Therefore take heed to yourselves and to all the flock, among which the Holy Spirit has made you overseers, to shepherd the church of God which He purchased with His own blood. For I know this, that after my departure savage wolves will come in among you, not sparing the flock. Also from among yourselves men will rise up, speaking perverse things, to draw away the disciples after themselves. Therefore watch, and remember that for three years I did not cease to warn everyone night and day with tears."[1]

He told the churches of Galatia, "I marvel that you are turning away so soon from Him who called you in the grace of Christ, to a different gospel, which is not another; but there are some who trouble you and want to pervert the gospel of Christ. But even if we, or an angel from heaven, preach any other gospel to you than what we have preached to you, let him be accursed."[2]

The heresy Paul was referring to was the Heresy of the Judaizer. By putting their faith in a ritual instead of the blood Christ shed on the cross for sinners, this error was canceling out true salvation by faith alone—which is given as the only way to heaven in both the Old Testament[3] and the New Testament.[4]

Some Jews from Judea did not understand that it was prophesied in the Old Testament that

---

[1] Acts 20:28-31
[2] Galatians 1:6-7
[3] Genesis 15:6
[4] Romans 1:17

the ritual of physical circumcision was to become a spiritual circumcision of the heart under the new covenant. They insisted physical circumcision as found in the Old Testament was also to be performed under the New Testament. How difficult it must have been for the Apostle Paul to explain that, yes, the shedding of blood in the little boy's circumcision was a necessary and symbolic part of the old covenant; but under the new covenant, Jesus' blood fulfilled that part of the law and had been shed for all—therefore the shedding of blood in circumcision was no longer necessary.

In fact, it was making Christ's blood shed on the cross of no effect if the Judaizer continued to do it. Even worse, the Bible says it would have caused them to fall from grace; i.e., lose their salvation:

> "Indeed I, Paul, say to you that if you become circumcised, Christ will profit you nothing. And I testify again to every man who becomes circumcised that he is a debtor to keep the whole law. You have become estranged from Christ, you who attempt to be justified by law; you have fallen from grace."
> (Galatians 5:2–4)

So serious did the early Church consider the Heresy of the Judaizer that the first Church council ever called was convened in Jerusalem to deal with this error. The apostle Peter spoke before the gathering, sharing with the assembled leadership (including Jesus' other disciples) that

God had already accepted the Gentiles at Cornelius's house without a ritual.[5] So, after much discussion, a conclusion was made: a ritual is not necessary for salvation, and that if one believes that salvation comes through a ritual, they have set aside the grace of God.

> "I do not set aside the grace of God; for if righteousness comes through the law [a ritual], then Christ died in vain."
> (Galatians 2:21, emphases added)

At that time, a letter was drafted to the churches from the Jerusalem Council that stated that a ritual was not necessary for salvation. It was circulated to all the churches of Galatia and eventually ended up in a book in the New Testament:

> "Since we heard that some who went out from us have troubled you with words, unsettling your souls, saying, "You must be circumcised and keep the law"—to whom we gave no such commandment—it seemed good to us, being assembled with one accord, to send chosen men to you with our beloved Barnabas and Paul...who will also report the same things by word of mouth."
> (Acts 15:24–25, 27)

That should have clinched the matter. The question had been openly discussed. The Church elders and apostles believed they had the mind of the Lord on the matter and had dealt with it decisively. The Judaizers, however, would not let the

---

[5] Acts 10

matter lie even after those at the Jerusalem Council, composed of Jesus' disciples as well as elders of the Church, had made their joint ruling.

However, the Judaizers continued to interrupt Paul's missionary journeys and physically attacked him because he insisted on preaching that a ritual was not to be a part of new covenant Christianity. When the apostle wrote the New Testament book of Galatians, he found it necessary to teach on this problem again. He said, "O foolish Galatians! Who has bewitched you that you should not obey the truth, before whose eyes Jesus Christ was clearly portrayed among you as crucified? This only I want to learn from you: Did you receive the Spirit by the works of the law, or by the hearing of faith?"[6]

The Judaizer was choosing to keep all of the more than six hundred Old Testament laws perfectly, including the ritual of circumcision. By insisting that a ritual was necessary for salvation, they were reverting back to the old covenant (circumcision is a ritual of Old Testament law) for their salvation. The old covenant, however, was no longer in effect because Jesus' blood had ratified the new covenant.

This heresy was only one of the many heresies that would come against Christianity during its first centuries. During those years, in subtle ways, Old Testament Judaism would become as much a threat to the purity of the gospel as

---

[6] Galatians 3:1-2

would the paganism found in the mystery, goddess religions that covered the Roman Empire at that time.

Both Judaism and the pagan religions considered Christianity an enemy to their old way of doing business. Although there were those from both sides who were drawn to Christianity, there also were those from both groups who wanted Christianity's benefits without completely giving up their old ways. These chose to enter the new Church and take on the Christian name without fully embracing its teachings.

Many heresies would spring up in the young Church as a result of mixing Christian practices with pagan practices. Those from Old Testament Judaism who wanted to keep the ritual of circumcision of infants, believing that circumcision saves, contributed to this error, as did those from the goddess religions who wanted to retain the mystery religions' belief that baptism saves. Together, these two errors would eventually meld into a new ritual of baptizing infants—even calling it a form of Old Testament circumcision. Thus did the Heresy of the Judaizer enter the Christian church.

How very conveniently this new ritual would begin to gain theological acceptance as a thinly-veiled type of Old Testament circumcision, even though it was nothing more than the Judaizers' warmed-over error in believing that circumcision saves recycled into a baptism of infants and expressed through baptismal regeneration.[7] For those in the Church who accepted this error, the Blood of Christ was immediately made of no effect.

Today theologians still debate on the subject of the Heresy of the Judaizer. Some believe that it never materialized and are surprised that a council needed to be called to deal with it. Others believe that it was very serious but that it was effectively dealt with at that time. This can be seen in their critiques of the subject.

John Polhill argues that the Heresy of the Judaizer was very serious. In *Paul and His Letters*, he states that the apostle Paul "was absolutely livid" over the Heresy of the Judaizer. Accusing the Galatians of being foolish for accepting the error, he stated they would pay the penalty on Judgment Day because they were alienating themselves from Christ.[8]

Robert H. Gundry, in *A Survey of the New Testament,* agrees. He states that fewer and fewer Gentiles would have converted to Christ if the error had not been addressed.[9] Jack W. Hayford, editor of *Hayford's Bible Handbook,* concurs. He believes the Heresy of the Judaizer was a serious contradiction of the gospel and in direct opposition to the teaching of salvation by faith alone.[10]

---

[7] Genesis 15–17; Acts 15
[8] John Polhill, *Paul and His Letters* (Nashville, TN: B & H Publishing Group, 1999), 138.
[9] R. H. Gundry, *A Survey of the New Testament*, 318.
[10] Jack W. Hayford, *Hayford's Bible Handbook,* 637.

Merrill F. Unger, ThD, PhD, of *Unger's Bible Dictionary,* flatly stated that the Judaizers were not really Christians at all![11]

But the secret that even these learned theologians have missed and that I would also have missed if the Lord had not given me a word was that the Heresy of the Judaizer is not just a long-forgotten theological event in Church history. It is very much present in today's Church. Although the heresy has mutated slightly—from a ritual of circumcision to a ritual of baptism—it is still deceiving much of the Church world today and causing many to go into a godless eternity.

The Heresy of the Judaizer—a belief that one can be saved through a ritual—is not only found in the infant baptism churches. It is also found worldwide in religions, such as Hinduism. The Hindus believe that baptism saves and that they become immortal when they are twice-born through dipping in the Ganges River.[12]

The belief that baptism saves is also found in cults such as the Latter-Day Saints (Mormon) Church. With Christ as a mere figurehead and Christianity a camouflage, Mormons baptize even dead people, believing they are saved in baptism. They teach that if they do enough good works, including proxy baptism of the dead, they will become a god when they die, marry numerous goddess wives, and have their own planet, which

---

[11] Merrill F. Unger, *Unger's Bible Dictionary,* 469.
[12] http://www.asiagrace.com

they will populate with multitudes of spirit children.[13]

Thus, the Heresy of the Judaizer—believing salvation comes through observing a ritual—has led many people into deception.

---

[13] Ed Decker, "The Law of Eternal Progression," Saints Alive in Jesus, http://www.saintsalive.com/mormonism/eternalprogression.htm (accessed September 2, 2008). See also Paul Bucknell, "Dangers of Mormon Cult Teachings," Biblical Foundations for Freedom, http://www.foundationsforfreedom.net/Topics/Belief/Mormonism.html

8

LUTHER'S FLIP-FLOP

When Luther finally discovered what Jesus meant when He informed Nicodemus, the rich young ruler, that one must be born again, he was stunned. He wondered that salvation could be that easy. He said the gates of paradise seemed to open up to him when he finally succeeded in grasping the simplicity of the gospel, that "the just shall live by faith" (Rom. 1:17).

Some may frown on the term and prefer to call it simply "Luther's tower experience." But on one thing all can agree: he had uncovered the biblical way of salvation long hidden by the official state Church of his day.

Luther himself didn't worry about terminology. Every chance he got, he broadcast to the world around him that when he gave up trying to get to heaven through good works and placed himself in the hands of a merciful God, his faith in only the blood of Jesus brought reconciliation with God. Peace flooded his soul.[1]

---

[1] Heiko A. Oberman, *Luther: Man Between God and the Devil* (New Haven, CT: Yale University Press, 1989), 153. See also WAT 6. No.6647; 95, 14–18.

Luther had come into agreement with the New Testament truth that salvation is by faith alone and not by any works of man, "For in it the righteousness of God is revealed from faith to faith; as it is written, the just shall live by faith."[2] It also states in Romans 3:28, that: "Therefore we conclude that a man is justified by faith apart from the deeds of the law."

Faith is also the way of salvation under the old covenant, for it was not Abraham's circumcision that saved him—it was his faith! Habakkuk 2:4 states, "…the just shall live by his faith."

Unfortunately, after Luther was reprimanded at the Diet of Worms and a ban was placed on his life, he moved away from his earlier revelation. Oh, he still mouthed the words, but he taught a different gospel. In place of "faith alone," he allowed "baptism saves" to be put in the Augsburg Confession.

The Bible warns against changing the gospel. The Apostle Paul stated that even if an angel from heaven should come preaching a gospel other than the one he and his team were preaching, they would be eternally condemned, because a perverted gospel is no gospel at all.[3]

As the years passed, Luther seemed to forget that his own early years were miserable and full of anxiety because he knew he was not right with God, even though he had been baptized as an in-

---

[2] Romans 1:17
[3] Galatians 1:6–9

fant. Before the Diet of Worms, he had written about many lovely and true things from the Bible. We read of his zeal that the peasants might know the true way of salvation as he had when he had his famous revelation. He was angry at his mother Church because they were telling the peasants the way to heaven was earned through good deeds and buying forgiveness.

On the night before Halloween in 1517 Luther declared enough is enough! He marched up to the Wittenberg church and nailed his famous "Ninety-five Theses" to the church door. It was his call for reformation within his large and rich Church! Later he would write an important paper called "An Address to the Christian Nobility," which gave his opinion on what would happen to those who believed a work or ritual was necessary for salvation.[4] Although he did not use the term Heresy of the Judaizer, a term coined much later in theological circles, he described the error by saying that anyone who attempts to become righteous by works will fall from grace:

> "From this anyone can clearly see how a Christian man is free from all things and over all things, so that he needs no works to make him righteous and to save him since faith alone confers all these things abundantly. But should he grow so foolish as to presume to become righteous, free, saved, and a Christian by means of some good work, he would in that instant lose

---

[4] Galatians 5:2–4

faith and all its benefits."[5]

But as time went on, Martin Luther's passion faded. He still shouted against the Roman Catholic Church, calling them names but, in fact, he was back with them doctrinally. He would after that teach through his writings that infant baptism is necessary for salvation and that "baptism saves." He turned away from his reliance on faith alone. He added infant baptism as also the way to heaven. His new dependence on infant baptism stopped the Reformation cold.

There were now two sets of Luther's teachings out there, and no one seemed to notice—the one that set the beleaguered peasant free and gave them a converted heart—that of salvation by faith alone—and the teaching of their prior church that salvation comes through a ritual, the Heresy of the Judaizer.

Luther had been deceived. He failed to complete the task of purifying the mother Church. This was not unusual. Other godly leaders also failed when they tried to rid their nation of the idolatry that was being practiced within their borders. God acknowledged that their hearts were right, but they failed to do the full council of God.

Example 1

> "Asa did what was right in the eyes of the Lord, as did his father David. And he banished the per-

---

[5] Martin Luther: "*A Treatise on Christian Liberty,*" *Three Treatises* (Philadelphia, PA: Muhlenberg Press, 1947), 51.

verted persons from the land, and removed all the idols that his fathers had made. Also he removed Maachah his grandmother from being queen mother, because she had made an obscene image of Asherah...But the high places were not removed. Nevertheless Asa's heart was loyal to the Lord all his days."

(1 Kings 15:11–14)

Example 2

"Jehoshaphat...walked in all the ways of his father Asa. He did not turn aside from them, doing what was right in the eyes of the Lord. Nevertheless the high places were not taken away, for the people offered sacrifices and burned incense on the high places."

(1 Kings 22:41, 43)

Example 3

"And he [Amaziah] did what was right in the sight of the Lord, yet not like his father David; he did everything he as his father Joash had done. However, the high places were not taken away, and the people still sacrificed and burned incense on the high places."

(2 Kings 14:3–4)

These are scriptural examples of godly men who were blinded to the need to tear down the places where idolatry was being practiced in their land and thus failed to complete their task. They show the subtlety with which Satan can implant or suggest a slight variation from truth, which will eventually ruin a whole nation or church. These Old Testament kings attempted to purge their nation of false religion but failed to get rid of all the places where it was practiced. This eventually led their nation back into sin.

That is what happened to Martin Luther. He fell into the same trap as others before him. Before the Reformation, he preached loudly and clearly that salvation is by faith alone. Later, he reversed himself. In place of "saved by faith," he allowed infant baptism and "baptism saves" to be written into Lutheran Church doctrine, Thus, the Heresy of the Judaizer spread into the Protestant daughter churches that accepted infant baptism.

As for Martin Luther, he had fallen victim to the dreaded Heresy of the Judaizer, and like everything else he did, he wholeheartedly embraced it.

> "The baptismal service was also translated into German, for Luther wished to make the parents of those baptized aware of the importance of this sacrament, by means of which the infant became regenerated, was delivered from the devil, sin, and death and was made a member of the Christian communion of saints."[6]

John Agricola, a contemporary of Luther's, noted that Luther had strayed from his original God-given revelation of faith alone. He tried to bring it to Luther's attention—and to the attention of the other Reformation leaders—but it only

---

[6] Harold J. Grimm, *The Reformation Era* (New York: Macmillan, 1973), 126.

made Luther furious. Luther threatened to put a ban on Agricola's life similar to the one the Roman Catholic Church had earlier placed on his life at the Diet of Worms. This meant anyone could kill him on sight and at will, without any civic or, supposedly, eternal penalty. The ban could have meant Agricola's death, had he not fled the country before Luther could put his threat into action.[7]

Few modern historians have noted this flip-flop, so enamored have they been of the five hundred year old memory of Martin Luther. His early teachings of salvation by faith alone are known as the work of the young Luther and his later teachings, those of salvation by baptismal regeneration, as those of the old Luther. Today's Lutheran Church carries the teachings of the old Luther, although the cliché "salvation by faith alone" is often heard on Sunday mornings.

The Heresy of the Judaizer can be seen in the Lutheran Book of Worship where it says clearly that in the waters of infant baptism today's children are reborn.[8] The doctrinal change to "saved by infant baptism" was slipped into Lutheran Church doctrine in place of "saved by faith." This change did not originate with Luther but was penned by his best friend and longtime associate,

---

[7] Bernhard Lohse, *Martin Luther* (Philadelphia, PA: Fortress Press, 1986), 202.
[8] Inter-Lutheran Commission on Worship, *The Lutheran Book of Worship* (Minneapolis, MN: Augsburg Publishing House, 1978), 121.

Philip Melanchthon.

Philip Melanchthon is known as the Lutheran theologian in today's seminaries because he wrote most of the doctrine of the Lutheran Church. He inserted "baptism saves" into a doctrinal paper he wrote for a special meeting called between the Catholic and the Lutheran Churches. The purpose of this meeting was to search for common ground upon which to reconcile.

The paper Melanchthon wrote for this meeting is familiar to most people today as the Augsburg Confession. Today the Augsburg Confession is the foundation of Lutheran doctrine. In it, Melanchthon replaced Luther's famous reformation-starting revelation of salvation by faith alone, with "baptism saves." Many think he did this in an effort to curry favor with the Roman Catholic Church, with whom he secretly hoped to reunite.[9]

Another possible reason Melanchthon placed "baptism saves" in the Augsburg Confession in place of "saved by faith" is because he was deeply involved in astrology, and the belief that "baptism saves" and astrology run hand in hand. Luther was aware of Melanchthon's involvement with astrology but seemed unconcerned that it might bring deception into the new church Luther was starting.

Luther chided Melanchthon on his dependence

---

[9] Theodore G. Tappert, *The Book of Concord* (Minneapolis, MN: Augsburg Publishing House, 1959), 13.

on astrology. He thought it was humorous that Melanchthon would not make even minor decisions without consulting his horoscope. For example, one time just before Luther's death, Melanchthon delayed their return home, even though Luther was not feeling well, until his horoscope lined up with their travel plans.[10]

It was because Melanchthon relied on astrology—not the Bible—that he wanted to keep baptismal regeneration as the theology of any church in which he took part. Of Greek descent himself, Melanchthon was a professor of Greek and Roman culture at the Wittenberg University and was immersed in Greek history and languages, as well as thoroughly steeped in the goddess religions which come out of Greek and Roman mythology, which embrace both astrology and the belief that "baptism saves."[11]

Philip Melanchthon has gained the reputation of being the Lutheran theologian in contemporary seminaries today because he wrote more of the Lutheran Church doctrine than did Martin Luther. It is time to examine the doctrine he selected for it way back in the 1500s. This will allow members of that church (and other infant baptism churches) to determine whether the things

---

[10] H. G. Haile, *Luther* (Princeton, NJ: Princeton University Press, 1983), 215; Oberman, 330. See also WAT 5. No. 5368, Summer 1540; K. Martin Luther's Werke: Kritsche Gesamtausgabe Tischreden (Table Talk) Vols. 1–6 (Weimar, 1912-21).
[11] Haile, 215; Oberman, 330.

they are being taught today line up with what the New Testament says. Otherwise, we don't have a Church; we just have one more world religion.

The belief system of any cult is accepted by its members because they do not understand the truth about God's blood covenant, nor do they understand the importance of the shed blood of Jesus Christ. Many seek peace with God but lack doctrinal foundations as did Luther in his youth.

They have no basic road map to follow because they have not been allowed (or have not chosen to) read the Bible. This makes them prime targets for facsimiles of Christianity, religions which may look authentic and even have Christ as figurehead, but which deny the saving power of the blood of Christ by teaching that "baptism saves."

Currently the infant baptism churches are elevating infant baptism to the same level as Christ's shed blood on the cross. If the Lutheran Church (and other infant baptism denominations) do not wish to fall into the same category as false religions, it is necessary for them to change their doctrines to agree with the Bible.

9

NOAH, THE GIANTS & INFANT BAPTISM

Infant baptism can be found in the Roman Catholic church with its 1.2 billion followers and in the many Protestant churches that also teach a baptism of infants. Because the Bible does not teach a baptism of infants, I began researching the origins of infant baptism.

I soon discovered that baptism, as their hope for gaining eternal life, is also found in pagan religions including, but not limited to, the Mystery religions, Sun worship, Hinduism and the Mormon/Latter Day Saints cult with Hindus and Mormons even baptizing the dead.

In researching the origins of the belief that "baptism saves", one might be tempted to believe it goes back to the false religion originally started at the Tower of Babel (Gen.10-11). But it actually goes further back in time to a misrepresentation of the Noah and the great flood incident as found in Genesis 6-9.

There are those who scoff at the possibility of a major occurrence such as a flood covering the whole world. But there is much scientific evidence that such a flood did really occur; even remnants of the ark have been sighted and procured.[1] Archeologists dig up fossils showing the sudden demise of animals caught in a state of catastrophe as rain began to fall.

A professor at a nearby college routinely scoffed at Christianity in his "Developing a Philosophy of Life" class. Noah and the flood account was one of his major targets. The Bible, he would say at the beginning of each semester, is just a book of myths like those found in all other world religions. According to him, the Bible was nothing more than folklore. He pointed out that almost all world religions and literature contain some version of a flood story which, in his worldview, made Noah nothing special.

I was in class one day when he began expounding this opinion. A new student's hand shot up. "Sir," the question was asked, "have you considered the possibility that the flood account might be true—that where there is so much smoke—maybe there really was a fire?"

The prepared student then began to read a footnote from the Amplified Bible. It said that in 1606, a man named P. Jansen of Hoorn, Holland, produced a model of the ark fashioned after the pattern God gave Noah in Genesis 6:14-16.[2]

The discovery was made that the pattern for the ark that God gave Noah was wonderfully seaworthy. The vessel was light, waterproof, com-

---

[1] www.noahsark-naxuan.com/1.htm
[2] KJV Amplified Holy Bible-Parallel Bible. 10

fortable, well-ventilated and perfectly planned to be large enough to accommodate the original land animals as well as four couples for the duration of the flood and the drying out period that followed. In fact, it could carry one-third more cargo than any other ship of similar cubical proportions.

According to the Registry of Shipping, World Almanac,[3] Jansen's model of the ark revolutionized shipbuilding and the world's navies. After 1609 when the model was made, ocean-going ships began to be patterned after the biblical rendering of God's blueprint given Noah to build the ark, for it was beautifully designed and "well-adapted for floating."

The design of the world's ships only changed again later after vessels became engine-driven and needed a contour designed to be more conducive to speed—a matter of no particular concern to Noah. The professor conceded, and wondered why no one had ever told him that before.

The fact that the biblical rendering of Noah and the Ark is accurate is no surprise to Bible readers who have long believed that Noah was a real human being and that a flood covered the earth in his day. The Bible teaches that Noah alone was righteous of all the people who were alive on the earth at that time.[4] So he was righteous in the eyes of God long before God gave him the in-

---

[3] Ibid.
[4] Genesis 6-8

structions that would allow him to build the ark that saved him and his family from destruction when the big flood came.

Elsewhere in the Bible, Noah is called "the preacher."[5] It is easy to picture him, the one righteous man among multitudes of wicked men, women and children, admonishing his fellow citizens to get right with God and to stop their evil ways. But the people would not give heed and their wickedness so grieved God that He unleashed a gigantic flood that would cover the whole earth and rid it of evil.

God told Noah how to build the huge boat that would save him and his family. Having been given instruction for the ship design, Noah was instructed upon its completion to take on board his wife, three sons and their wives, plus male and female of the various species.

God Himself closed the door when Noah's family and the animals were safely on board. When they emerged from the ark many months later, Noah immediately fell on his knees in gratefulness to God for keeping them safe. He hurried to make preparation to build an altar and there he sacrificed several animals in a burnt offering of thanksgiving.

Generations and centuries went by, and Noah's descendants strived to keep alive the account of their forefather—the one so important that the God of this earth made special arrangements to

---

[5] II Peter 2:5

save his life when all others perished. They told and retold of him safely navigating a huge boat through the waters of a flood that ravaged every other creature and every blade of grass.

Unfortunately, Noah's descendants soon forgot that God had been good to their ancestor because, and only because, of his righteousness. Otherwise he and his family would have perished like everyone else. They began to build Noah up as some great hero who had outwitted God and saved himself. They minimized his righteous walk before God and instead idolized him as a man who had safely navigated the waters of a great flood; a man who had successfully contended with God and brought his family to safety when God planned evil upon him and the whole world.

Intentionally or unintentionally, a false religion was born. The fact that God Himself gave Noah the plan for safekeeping because of his righteousness was passed over as his descendants' minds darkened. They gave credit to Noah as having saved himself and seven others by craftiness when God sent the great deluge. Soon a belief evolved that passing safely through the waters was a symbolic way to gain God's favor and go to heaven. Their false belief caused a breach between man and God.

The myths surrounding Noah's prowess expanded. One example of the retelling of the Noah event is the early Gilgamesh epic studied worldwide in most college ancient literature classes. On Tablet XI, it relates a flood story similar to

Noah's in the Babylonian traditions. In it, Utnapishtim plays the part of Noah and, like Noah; he survives cosmic destruction by heeding divine orders to build an ark.[6]

In correlation with this falsification, other phenomena occurred that taken together would further remove a relationship with God from men's minds. The Bible includes the account in abbreviated form and it's almost too much for contemporary man to handle—though many stories and motion pictures try to wrap our minds around it so as to make sense of it.

> "Now it came to pass, when men began to multiply on the face of the earth, and daughters were born to them, that the sons of God saw the daughters of men, that they were beautiful; and they took wives for themselves of all whom they chose....There were giants on the earth in those days, and also afterward, when the sons of God came in to the daughters of men and they bore children to them. Those were the mighty men who were of old, men of renown."
>
> (Genesis 6:1-4)

The myths about Noah became intertwined with mankind's fascination with the fathering of these half angelic/half human beings. The offspring of these supernatural beings would be giants, men of renown, including Goliath the giant who was killed by the shepherd boy David. Four

---

[6] "Noah" Encyclopaedia Britannica *online:* www.search.eb.com/bol/topic?eu=57401&sctn=1 [accessed 18 September 2001]

sons of one giant are mentioned as being killed by David's mighty men. Two of their names were Ishbi-Benob and Saph, (II Sam. 21:16; II Sam. 21:18).

People were curious about these facts and many myths would grow in the imaginations of men. The Greek classics, by such poets as Homer, are tales written about the deeds and misdeeds of these angelic beings, with a fictitious domicile assigned them on Mt. Olympus. Out of these imaginings came stories of mythological exploits that account for the god/ goddesses of Greek and Roman mythology as well as Hinduism, the mystery religions, sun worship and certain aspects found in Mormonism (LDS) as well.

The names of their deities multiplied because of the language confusion at the Tower of Babel and include such names as Isis, Artemis, Astarte, Aphrodite, Asheroth, Athena and Diana for the "goddesses" as well as a variety of names given to their sons/cohorts, including the various Baals and one in particular named Tammuz.

The New Testament continues the account of the fallen angels. We are told that God chained, in darkness under the earth, the angelic beings who conjoined with earth women and fathered the giants. These fallen angels are referred to as the angels "who left their first estate."

There is no indication that all of the fallen angels who followed Satan in his rebellion joined in this activity but those that did remain God's prisoners. They are being held in darkness until Judgment Day where they will, no doubt, receive harsh judgment for starting the false religions that spread worldwide, leading multitudes away from redemption and a relationship with the true God:

> "For if God did not spare the angels who sinned, but cast them down to hell and delivered them into chains of darkness, to be reserved for judgment...."
>
> (2 Peter 2:4-6)
>
> "And the angels who did not keep their proper domain, but left their own abode, He has reserved in everlasting chains under darkness for the judgment of the great day...."
>
> (Jude 1: 6)

The Bible warns against fallen angelic beings who bring false religions. It says, "But even if we, or an angel from heaven, preach any other gospel to you than what we have preached to you, let him be accursed."[7] Unfortunately, there are two religions today that were given at different times by fallen angels to two illiterate men, Mohammed and Joseph Smith, Jr.

In 610 A.D., Mohammed met with an angel in a cave and was given "a holy book" and told to start the Islam religion. Its purpose was to displace Christianity.[8] In 1823, the Mormon church (LDS) was started by another angel, Moroni, in a cave. Joseph Smith, Jr. said he, too, was told to start Mormonism to displace Christianity.[9]

---

[7] Galatians 1:8
[8] www.allaboutreligion.org/Origin-Of-Islam.htm
[9] www.exmormon.org/tract2.htm

If one hesitates to accept angelic interference in religion, consider, for example, the similarities found in these two religions, Islam and the Mormon (LDS) church, which seem more than mere coincidence. Coming from the same source, this would be expected.[10]

- Both started by fallen angels.
- Both men to whom the angels appeared were (or claimed to be) illiterate.
- Both men visited by angelic beings in a cave.
- Both men given religious books.
- Both men told their new religion was going to replace Old Testament Judaism and New Testament Christianity.
- Both men told that Jesus was not God
- Both men told that Jesus was a prophet
- Both teach polygamy.
- Both teach multiple sexual partners after death.
- Both worship Allah (Islam openly; Mormons in the high echelons of their religion).
- Both murdered "infidels" on 9/11. Mormons in the Mountain Meadows Massacre - 1857 Utah and Islamists in the Twin Towers Disaster - 2001 New York.

While stories of beings in the atmosphere seem

---

[10] www.bible.ca/islam/islamic-mormonism-similarities.htm www.bible.ca/islam/islamic-mormonism-similarities.htm findarticles.com/p/articles/mi_qn4188/is_20110313/ai_n57069290/ www.uvu.edu/religiousstudies/mormonismandislam/

ridiculously farfetched in today's realistic way of thinking, we can nonetheless see traces of how these belief systems emerged to become the mystery religions of Greece, Rome, Asia, and beyond.

Even today we see women promoting the concept of "Sophia," first at the "RE-imagining" conferences and, more recently, in small groups within several of the churches that sponsored these conferences. Most in the infant baptism churches are not aware that a similar belief system is at the root of most pagan religions—the belief that "baptism saves"—and which emerged as a result of the misinterpretation of the Noah and the ark account.[11]

If we could not see that there really are mythological gods and goddesses in such religions as sun worship, Hinduism and the mystery religions, our western mindset would likely just dismiss all this as silliness. But—though unusual—these are the events that can be traced back to most of the false religions currently in the world today.[12]

All this "goddess stuff" has brought great distrust to the worship of the one true God, especially among intellectuals. And who can blame them for embracing philosophy—a study of what man thinks about these things—as they attempt to understand God and their beginnings? But by

---

[11] See *The Secret About Infant Baptism That Everyone's Missing.* Amazon.com

[12] Anderson, Sir Norman. *Christianity and World Religions.* Leicester, England: InterVarsity Press, 1984, 65.

using secondary sources instead of the Bible, which is a primary source and has writings that go back in history for thousands of years with scores of impeccable authors inspired by God, they only deepen their unbelief.

A respected book to consult regarding the false god/goddess intrusion into Christianity through the Noahic myth is *The Two Babylons*, a book by the Rev. Alexander Hislop. His research authenticates much of the history of the god/goddess beliefs that are known collectively as the Mystery Religions and is foundational to much of the following information:

Hislop says that in India, land of a million gods, the main "god" is known by the name Vishnu, meaning "the Preserver." Vishnu's story is similar to Noah's in that he is credited with being supernaturally preserved along with a single righteous family when great worldwide flooding occurred, drowning the rest of the world. In Sanskrit, Vishnu means Noah. In Chaldean, the word for Noah is similar: "Ish-nuh" means "Man of rest."[13]

When the Adamic race spread worldwide after their failed attempt to build the Tower of Babel,[14] the masses having been dispersed when God divided them into people groups through the use of various languages,[15] the name of their deities

---

[13] Ibid. 59 (Also Wilson's India Three Thousand Years Ago)
[14] Genesis 11:1-10
[15] Genesis 10, 11.

would also mutate slightly.[16] Yet goddess worship had been established by the residents of Babel and would remain shockingly similar.[17]

The names of the original priest and priestess at the tower of Babel were Nimrod and Semiramas. According to books on ancient Greek and Roman religions, after Nimrod died his widow Semiramas claimed that a son, Tammuz, was conceived by a sunbeam. She declared that her husband was now a sun god in heaven. This, according to her, made her baby son a sun god and she, herself, became queen of heaven and mother of God![18]

This has resulted in a religion with an emphasis on the mother as she protected and cared for her baby son. Ancient art focuses on this relationship, often having golden rays emanating from the heads of the main characters; thus did a sun god and "queen of heaven-type" worship evolve in many regions of the world. Examples are Fortuna and Jupiter; Isis and Horus[19] and, of course, it infiltrated the church at Rome in the form of Madonna and son with Madonna (or Mary) also given the same titles of "mother of

---

[16] Rives, Richard M. *Too Long in the Sun*. (Partakers Publications, Charlotte, NC. 1997, 51-76; The Zondervan Pictorial Encyclopedia of the Bible, Vol. 3, 334.

[17] Hislop, A. *The Two Babylons*. Neptune, NJ: Loizeaux Brothers, 1916, 132; Bonnefay. *246;* Davies. 69.

[18] Ibid.

[19] Hislop, A. *The Two Babylons*. Neptune, NJ: Loizeaux Brothers, 1916; 140. (Also Pompeii, vol. ii. P.150)

God" and "Queen of heaven."[20]

Most Christians unwittingly enter into observances with the sun god and goddesses of mythology when they celebrate the birthday of Jesus as occurring on December 25th, This is the same date chosen by the pagan world for a birthday celebration of their sun god. Long before the Roman Catholic church adopted that date as the birthday of Jesus, it was celebrated in mid-eastern nations as the birthday of the sun god, including Zeus, Tammuz, Ra and Mithra (Mithra is the name under which the sun god entered Rome and became Rome's official state religion).

When the Roman Empire conquered Jerusalem, it was "the cross of Mithra" upon which they hung Jewish patriots. The date they did this was December 25th and they did it as a sacrifice to their sun god.[21] Can things get worse? Ever wonder why, during Lent, one mourns forty days before Jesus' death on the cross? This practice of mourning before Jesus' death can be traced back to the goddess religions, also.

As the myth goes, Tammuz, a sun god/fertility god, was gored by a wild boar and died. He descended into the netherworld. His mother searched for him (some versions say it was his consort, Ishtar). She finally found him but with his reproductive organ missing. She mourns for

---

[20] Hunt, D. *A Woman Rides the Beast.* Eugene, OR: Harvest House Publishers, 1994, 430. (also Wagner, 31.) Ezekiel 8:14; Jeremiah 7:18.
[21] Ruud, 61-62.

forty days as she searches the netherworld for the lost organ. On earth, pagan women, too, were celebrating a season of mourning (40 days) because all fertility ceased.

On the fortieth day, the lost is found and the two ascend back upon earth amidst immoral revelry at a festival that honors Ishtar. Today, we call it Easter![22] Another "Easter" myth has Ishtar falling to earth in a giant egg, hence today's celebrations of bunnies and eggs.

The book of Ezekiel tells of God's anger over the fact that Jewish women were also taking part in this festival.[23]

> "So He brought me to the door of the north gate of the Lord's house; and to my dismay, women were sitting there weeping for Tammuz...and they were worshiping the sun toward the east."
> (Ezekiel 8:14-16)

Another belief found in today's Christianity, that also has its roots in paganism, is the belief that one is saved in the waters of baptism. The belief that "baptism saves" originated with the occultic Chaldeans—the land of idolatry which Abraham, father of our faith, was told to leave. The Chaldeans initiated sun worship where, if one desired to become a follower of the sun god, they were required to first submit to a violently

---

[22] *The Zondervan Pictorial Encyclopedia of The Bible*, Vol.3, 334. Ruud, 65-66.
[23] Ezekiel 8:14

rigorous baptism.[24] If they survived the ordeal, they were promised "regeneration" and forgiveness of all past sins.[25]

The ancestors of today's Scandinavians also believed that 'baptism saves.' Worshipers of the pagan god Odin, they practiced a baptism of infants and believed that "the natural guilt and corruption of new-born children"[26] was washed away in a baptism of infants. Although it took their rulers 150-200 years to force Scandinavians to a half-hearted acceptance of Catholicism and later to Lutheranism—one thing remained stable—their practice of infant baptism. Any of their religions was only a stone's throw from what they had already been doing.[27]

Meanwhile in Mexico, half a world away, the practice of infant baptism, with its corresponding practice of baptismal regeneration, was also taking place. When the explorer Cortez discovered the Aztecs, he was surprised to find them baptizing babies. It was strikingly similar to what was already being performed by Roman Catholic missionaries.[28] There, too, the god Odin was being worshiped, as well as the queen of heaven who is also worshiped among the Chaldeans, Persians

---

[24] Bonnefay. 246; Davies. 69.
[25] Hislop. 132; (Also Eliase Comment. In 8. Greg. Naz., Orat. Iv.' Gredorii Nazanzine Opera, p.245)
[26] Ibid. *(Also Mallet on Anglo-Saxon Baptism, Antiquities, vol.i., p.335)*
[27] Ibid.
[28] Ibid. *(Humboldt's Mexican Researches, Vol.i., pp.185)*

and in the Canaanite religions.[29]

A Mexican[30] myth centers on Wodan (interchangeably called Odin), a grandson of Noah, who was saved on a raft when most of humanity perished in a great flood."[31] He is presented as one who cooperated in the construction of a great building undertaken by men to reach the skies.[32] Once more, we find evidence of the Noah story and its accompanying belief in baptismal regeneration.

Sooner or later someone will think to ask where a belief in baptizing babies comes from if "baptismal regeneration" through infant baptism is not a biblical principle. The scholar in the Roman and Greek mythological classics might immediately recognize the origins of this Roman Catholic doctrine of *"Limbo"* as originally coming from a poem titled *Aenid* that was written by Virgil a Roman poet.[33]

In *Aenid,* the story is told of a man named *Aeneas* who descends into the hot, sulphuric regions of hell. There he finds the souls of tormented infants. Death has cruelly snatched them from their mother's bosom before they could be given the "rites" of the church—that is, infant baptism!

---

[29] Ibid. *(Prescott's Mexico, Vol.iii. pp.339-340.)*
[30] Ibid. *According to the ancient traditions collected by Bishop Francis Nunez de la Vega.*
[31] Whyte. 32-33
[32] Ibid. *133. (Humboldt's Researches, Vol.I. p.320).*
[33] Hislop, 239. (Aeneid, Book vi.ll. 576-578, Dryden.—In Original, ll. 427-429)

"Before the gates the cries of babes new-born, whom fate had from their tender mothers torn, assault his ears."[34]

The epic goes on to speak of the horror of these "wretched babes" who have been eternally excluded from paradise (called the *Elysian Fields*) because their parents neglected to submit them to a ritual of infant baptism. Now, so the poem goes, they are to forever lay in torment alongside suicides who "prodigally threw their souls away."[35]

The Roman Catholic church adopted this myth as doctrine for their church (it is not found in the Bible) and it, understandably, put great fear into the soft hearts of parents who feared for their little ones. As a result, they hurried their offspring off to the Roman church which, they were taught, had the authority to properly minister the rites of baptism so their little son or daughter did not end up in hell's fire.

According to an article in the Minneapolis Star Tribune, the Pope changed his mind about this doctrine they called "Limbo." According to now Emeritus Pope Benedict, church offices were being swamped with calls having to do with the eternal destination of aborted babies. So on December 5, 2005, they issued a report to prepare the hearts of the faithful that a change was coming regarding Limbo.

---

[34] Aeneid, Book vi.ll. 576-578, Dryden.—In Original, ll. 427-429.
[35] Virgil, Book vi 586-589, Dryden's Translation. –Original, ll. 434-436.

> "For the unbelieving husband is sanctified by the wife, and the unbelieving wife is sanctified by the husband; otherwise your children would be *unclean*, but now they are *holy*."
>
> (I Corinthians 7:14, emphases added)

When one reads the previous verse, it is interesting to note that the root of God's declaration of our offspring as being "holy" is the same word *hagios* that is used for God's Holy Spirit. "Strong's Exhaustive Concordance of Bible Words: #40; Greek: *hagios.* Means physically pure; morally blameless or religious; consecrated; most holy; saints."[36]

Therefore, infant baptism is not necessary. God considers the offspring of believers' to be holy and not in need of any ritual to make them acceptable to Him should they die before the age of accountability.

---

[36] Also see No. 53; No. 2282.

PART II

INFANT BAPTISM CORRUPTS THE CHURCH

Then Peter said to them, "Repent, and let every one of you be baptized in the name of Jesus Christ for the remission of sins; and you shall receive the gift of the Holy Spirit.

—Acts 2:38

10

PURPLE SCARLET HARLOT

So the strikes against infant baptism were mounting *and it was about to get more serious*. Not only were there no Bible verses referring to a baptism of infants; it was a form of the dreaded *heresy of the Judaizer* for which the first ever Church council was called.

The early Church recognized the seriousness of this heresy because, as the Apostle Paul, said about the heresy of the Judaizer it would have changed the gospel to that which is no gospel at all! Only the ritual was changed. For this reason, we see today that the Church has two different branches, two different water baptisms and teaches two wildly-different ways for salvation.

In the infant baptism churches, most teach that "baptism saves." This belief is also taught I almost all false world religions including the Mystery Religions, Sun Worship, Hinduism and the Mormon cult of Church of Jesus Christ-Latter Day Saints. The Hindus and Mormons even baptize dead people.

So not only has the lie about infant baptism been used by the Roman Catholic church to deceive parents into believing they needed to baptize their infants into the Catholic church so they did not eternally suffer outside the gates of hell, they did it t cause distressed parents to rush to baptize their newborns and join them to the Roman Catholic church (as the only church that could "properly" baptize them). It was today's Emeritus Pope Benedict who debunked this myth in January of 2006.

The Apostle Paul, author of many of the books in the New Testament, had warned of coming apostasy in the church and, also true, he said those bringing apostasy into the church would be actual church members.

> "For I know this, that after my departure savage wolves will come in among you, not sparing the flock. Also from among yourselves men will rise up, speaking perverse things, to draw away the disciples after themselves. Therefore watch, and remember that for three years I did not cease to warn everyone night and day with tears."
> (Acts 20:29-31)

But someone even more important would warn of coming apostasy a short time later – it would be Jesus Christ, Himself. In a nighttime vision given to the Apostle John, Jesus warned him of coming apostasy but he actually went a step further – He actually identified the heresy! He said Satan would bring in a heresy about a false water baptism for the purpose of destroying the Church!

Jesus began by giving an overview of the Messiah's birth, death and resurrection. Then, encoded in just a few words, He warns of coming persecution against the Seed of the woman's followers:

> "Now when the dragon (Satan) saw that he had been cast to the earth, he persecuted the woman (God's people) who gave birth to the male *Child* (Jesus)."
>
> "But the woman was given two wings of a great eagle, that she might fly into the wilderness to her place, where she is nourished for a time and times and half a time[1] from the presence of the serpent."
>
> (Revelation 12:13-14, clarification added)

It was at this point that Jesus' warning becomes very specific. He not only warned of coming persecution but said the persecution would come against those who refused to practice Satan's lying baptism. By deceiving people into placing their trust in their baptism as an infant, they would put their faith in a ritual instead of in the atoning blood of Jesus Christ. Thus salvation would be circumvented—it would pervert the very thing Christ died to bring to mankind—the forgiveness of sins by His holy blood as well as the gift of the Holy Spirit.

So it bears repeating. It is to the believer's own peril that they scoff at prophetic words such as Jesus' nighttime vision given to the church. And it is in the next verse, that Jesus drops the

---

[1] Revelation 12:6

bombshell—Satan, the father of lies, would nearly destroy the church with a false water baptism!

> "Then from his mouth the serpent spewed water like a river, to overtake the woman (the church) and sweep her away with the torrent."
> (Revelation 12:15 NIV, clarification added)

His revelation continues. He tells His followers that God prepared a wilderness refuge for a remnant of believers for the purpose of preserving the gospel. In the northern Alps a remnant of the believing church lived for centuries amongst the rugged landscape of mountainous cliffs and raging rivers. Thus would "the earth" restrict the Roman Catholic church's access to believers hidden away out of their reach among the rough terrain. There, in relative peace, they could practice biblical Book of Acts Christianity without hindrance and also send teams to evangelize in the valleys below.

> "But the earth helped the woman by opening its mouth and swallowing the river that the dragon had spewed out of his mouth."
> (Revelation 12:16 NIV)

So in these verses, encoded in just a few brief words, the mystery of iniquity is laid bare! It was Satan himself who was riding the "beast," the Roman Empire, as he used them to systematically enable the "Roman church" to destroy New Testament believers. Enraged that they could not completely take down the little band of believers that sent evangelists undiscovered into the valleys below, the Roman Catholic church pursued the rest of Christ's followers:

> "Then the dragon was enraged at the woman [the church] and went off to make war against the rest of her offspring—those who obey God's commandments and hold to the testimony of Jesus."
>
> (Revelation 12:17 NIV, clarification added)

Satan, as "the serpent," infiltrated the Roman church. That is why the Old Testament prophet Daniel centuries before had seen a beast that was so terrible he was filled with horror. The beast had ten horns with a smaller one coming up in the middle of the others. It had a big mouth that spoke blasphemous things against God.[2]

Centuries later, John saw a similar beast in his vision. But in his vision, the beast was scarlet-colored and was being ridden by a harlot who was luxuriously clad in purple and scarlet and adorned with gold and pearls. In her hand was a golden goblet. In it was the filth leftover from her fornications.

> " ... And I saw a woman sitting on a scarlet beast which was full of names of blasphemy, having seven heads and ten horns. The woman was arrayed in purple and scarlet, and adorned with gold and precious stones and pearls, having in her hand a golden cup full of abominations and the filthiness of her fornication. And on her forehead a name was written: *MYSTERY, BABYLON*

---

[2] Daniel 7:7-21

THE GREAT, THE MOTHER OF HARLOTS AND OF THE ABOMINATIONS OF THE EARTH. I saw the woman, drunk with the blood of the saints and with the blood of the martyrs of Jesus. And when I saw her, I marveled with great amazement."
(Revelation 17:3-6)

This harlot was not an ordinary harlot—she was the "mother of harlots." Not only that, she was drunk on the blood of the saints! Biblical scholars still puzzle over who the harlot in John's vision represents. Some argue that it symbolizes the Jewish nation, since God Himself called Israel a harlot because of her involvement in idolatry before her exile to Babylon. However, it is unlikely this passage refers to the Jews because they have not returned to idolatry since their 70 years of chastisement in Babylon, 2,500 years ago.

For these reasons, certain scholars argue that the harlot is representative of a corrupted Christianity; in particular, the Roman Catholic church. They point out her co-mixture of pagan practices intermixed with Christianity and recall the millions killed by the Catholic church because they would not practice infant baptism. They also recall the decree that went out in 413 A.D. and again in 610 A.D. calling for death for those who remained faithful to the Book of Acts instructions to the new church, (Acts 2:38-39).

Yet hardly anyone has noted that the 'harlot' seen riding the scarlet beast is not an ordinary harlot—she is *"the mother"* of harlots! Therefore, riding (directing) the beast (which is the Roman

Empire) is the same false religion that caused the Old Testament Jew and the New Testament Christian to apostatize. She is called their "mother" because they have learned her ways. So it is likely the harlot referred to in the Revelation 17 passage—the wicked woman riding the scarlet beast—is neither Old Testament Judaism nor the New Testament Church but a false church which is really not a church at all but a wolf in sheep's clothing!

This *mother* of harlots that has corrupted both the Jews and the Church is actually a false religion disguised as the Church! The *Encyclopedia Britannica* concurs with this likelihood for it states that sun worship mysteriously disappeared from the Roman Empire at that time— *only to reappear in the church at Rome!*[3]

When did this happen? Again, according to the Encyclopedia Britannica, in the middle of the fourth century during the years when Constantine became emperor and other "christianized" emperors forced even pagan religions to join the church *and practice infant baptism!*[4]

---

[3] www.britannica.com/EBchecked/topic/507866/Roman-religion/65520/The-Sun-and-stars   www.end-times-prophecy.org/roman-catholic-sun-worship-eucharist.html
[4] Ibid.

11

ROME'S CERTIFICATE

Both the Old Testament prophecy in the Book of Daniel and the New Testament prophecy in the Book of Revelation point to the Roman Empire as enemies of God's people. This began to be evident almost immediately as the Roman government focused its rage on the new church:

> "And he shall speak great words against the Most High, and shall wear out the Saints of the Most High, and think to change times and laws: and they shall be given into his hand until a time and times and the dividing of time."
>
> (Daniel 7:25 KJV)

The Emperor Nero (54-68 A.D.) beheaded the Apostle Paul and crucified the Apostle Peter. He is said to have set Rome on fire, blaming the Christians. Persecutions by other emperors followed. The Emperor Aurelius (162 to 180 A.D.) crushed Christian's feet and then forced them to walk over thorns, nails and sharp objects. Others were whipped until veins and sinews were exposed.[1]

---

[1] Chadwick, Harold J. *The New Foxe's Book of Martyrs: Updated to include recent accounts from the 160,000 Martyred in 2001*. 11-37.

In 212 A.D., there was a brief respite for Christians while the Romans persecuted the Jews. This was short-lived and in 270 A.D., the Emperor Aurelian declared himself "God." The name he gave himself was Dominus et Deus, ruler of everything. Later this title would be passed down to future popes. The Church, however, grew and flourished during those first cataclysmic years. It was rapidly covering the Roman Empire and by the end of the middle of the fourth century, over fifty percent of the citizens of Rome had been genuinely converted.[2]

Now the Emperor Diocletian, a sun worshiper, rose up against the Christians. In A.D. 303, Diocletian began a persecution against Christians that included four edicts. His first edict commanded the destruction of all churches, the cessation of all worship and the burning of Scripture.

His second edict commanded all clergy be imprisoned; a third edict ordered all clergy to sacrifice to pagan gods on pain of death. The fourth edict commanded all laity to do likewise or suffer for their refusal.[3] Suddenly, in 305 A.D., the Emperor Diocletian abdicated the throne but the battle for the purity of the Church still raged—

---

[2] These estimates are based on 40 percent growth per decade, and roughly correspond with figures found in early church documents. For more details, see Rodney Stark, *The Rise of Christianity: A Sociologist Reconsiders History (Princeton, 1996).*
[3] Davies, J. G. *The Early Christian Church.* New York: Holt, Rinehart, and Winston, 1965. 118.

especially in North Africa—most of which refused to give up the authenticity of the Book of Acts salvation message.

Diocletian's sudden abdication left a vacancy in the throne room of the Roman Empire. Into this vacancy stepped a young man who was being trained up by his father to become the emperor of Rome!

12

KILLING CHRISTIANS OVER INFANT BAPTISM

Within fifty years after the Nicene Council, infant baptism (and the belief that "baptism saves") became an issue. Up until that time (378 A.D.), sun worship had been the official religion of the Roman Empire and one of the beliefs of sun worship was that "baptism saves."

When the *official* state religion of Rome changed from sun worship to "the church," the sun worship's belief that "baptism saves" was retained in the form of infant baptism. Faith in the atonement provided by Jesus' death as the only way of salvation was set aside.

All members of the Roman Empire were now ordered to join Rome's new church. To have one universal religion had been the intent of the emperors all along; thus had they succeeded with the result that even the pagan religions of Rome were now incorporated into "the church," official state religion of the Roman Empire! Thus was the name Roman *catholic (meaning universal)* church born.

However, the new *universal* religion of Rome

did not allow the instructions for the Church, as given by the apostle Peter on the Day of Pentecost, to be part of the new Roman church. The belief that "baptism saves" usurped faith in Jesus Christ while Mary was elevated (as mother of god and queen of heaven as in sun worship).

The Christians, who remained faithful disciples of Jesus Christ and followed the instructions given by the Apostle Peter, would not accept infant baptism and so were labeled heretics.

> "Then Peter said unto them, Repent, and be baptized everyone one of you in the name of Jesus Christ for the remission of sins, and ye shall receive the gift of the Holy Spirit."
> (Acts 2:38 KJV)

When the emperor became aware there were still individuals within his realm (and that of his brother Honorius) who continued to practice Christianity in the old-fashioned way, he was determined to destroy them. These believers refused to embrace infant baptism but went on about their business as usual, continuing to evangelize their friends and neighbors and baptizing them upon conversion.

This angered the emperors who wanted a uniform religion across their land. Now having the power to do something about it, the Roman emperors (it was not the Church) put forth their first death edict against those who refused to accept the doctrine that "baptism saves." They issued what came to be called the "bloody edict". It decreed death for those who refused to baptize their offspring and/or were rebaptized themselves.

The edict included the death of the one administering water baptism in the name of Jesus Christ for the forgiveness of sin. This meant the new believer was not given the opportunity to respond to God's offer of salvation by showing their faith through public baptism.[1]

> "The edict issued by the Emperors Theodosius and Honorius, reads thus: 'If any minister of the Christian church is found guilty of having rebaptized any one, he, together with the person thus rebaptized, provided the latter is proved to be of such an age as to understand the crime, shall be put to death.'"[2]

To the consternation of "the church," the later to be given the grandiose title of Roman Catholic (universal) Church, not all the churches under Rome's rule were doing as demanded. They continued to ignore infant baptism and followed New Testament instruction on baptizing only believers. So there continued to be large numbers of small churches throughout the empire that would not accept Rome's manmade tradition of infant baptism and the occult belief that 'baptism saves.'

This infuriated the Roman church. They had long been eyeing these churches with disfavor but could do nothing to bring them down be-

---

[1] van Braght. 198.
[2] Ibid.

cause it was evident to all that they were blooming in the midst of Roman debauchery. Persecution against the Church was rising. By the sixth century, fifteen major persecutions arose at the same time in twelve different countries including Arabia, Palestine, France, Italy, Africa, Armenia, Spain, and England.[3]

It was a concentrated, all-encompassing destruction aimed at destroying the true Church before it became embedded in society. Several nomadic tribes had been evicted from southern Russia, the Balkans and northern India and they now invaded Rome, raping and pillaging. This included the Visigoths, the Vandals, the Ostrogoths, the Gauls and Attila the Hun.

Having tried to dispel the marauders by force, Pope Leo I (440-461) tried a new tack. He opened wide his arms and offered baptismal membership to the thieving throng. They accepted and it brought the murderous rabble right into the inner circle of the church; some were even given positions of honor.

The smaller house churches were brought low by the vicious attacks of the barbarians; almost all having lost family members. Rome saw an opportunity to overtake these little groups in their weakened state. Taking advantage of the times, it harnessed every ounce of its remaining strength to charge after the Book-of-Acts-style churches.

Because of the brave Christians who dared to

---

[3] Ibid, 214.

preach true New Testament doctrine regardless of the cost, Rome was losing control over people's souls. This worried the papists who wanted to control the populace and aggrandize their coffers.

In a desperate effort to maintain control, they taught that in order to gain salvation people had to be baptized in the Roman Catholic church. Worried families rushed their newborns to the church to be baptized perchance they would lose their little one to an early death and be responsible for them being forced to exist forever in a state of the horror of the damned. It was cruel but it was effective.

In 606 A.D. something occurred that has since affected the Christian church. The bishop of Rome was made the ruler over all Christian churches—whether or not they practiced infant baptism. The title of Supreme Father was not given the Roman bishop by Jesus Christ or by God the Father. It was the secular Roman government (and not St. Peter) who conferred the grandiose title upon the bishop of the Roman church!

His name was Emperor Phocas and he conferred upon the bishop of the Roman church the title of Papa—meaning "pope" or Supreme Father. This gave the Catholic church a huge advantage in that day and age. The smaller house churches that had refused to come under Rome's jurisdiction were now in a treacherous position—it was either to succumb to Rome's false belief in infant baptism—or generally, be burned at the stake.

Pope Boniface III was the first to take advantage of the exalted title given the top man in the Catholic church. Finding himself in this new powerful position because of the decree, he ordered explicit obedience, stating all must baptize their infants. This removed salvation from the church because people were no longer repenting of their sins and receiving converted hearts and being baptized the Bible way.

> "[be it] established, decreed and published: That infants must be baptized, as necessary to their salvation."[4]

Next a law was made by the government of the Roman Empire that Christians would be killed if they did not baptize their infants.

> "We will, we ordain, we decree, we command, etc.; thus I will, thus I ordain, thus I decree, thus I command;" whereby many superstitions and human inventions were presented to the people as the Word of God; such as image worship, salutation of the sacrament, observance of infant baptism as necessary to salvation, etc....."[5]

The Roman Pope, as supreme head of the church, now had unlimited power and the practice of baptizing infants soon became so firmly entrenched that any who spoke against it were killed. The books and writings of pious believers were "lamentably and tyrannously"[6] destroyed so that no one would remember exactly what the "heresy" was for which the martyrs of the church

---

[4] Ibid.
[5] Ibid. 213.
[6] Ibid.

were being accused and burned at the stake.

However, books such as *Foxe's Book of Martyrs* and *Martyrs Mirror*, a three inch thick 8-1/2 x 11 inch book, escaped their clutches and a sampling of the names and groups of those murdered has been kept for posterity.[7] These groups included (but were not limited to) the following.

> "The poor men of Lyons, Chaignards (meaning dogs), Transmontani meaning (they had to cross the Alps to get away from their persecutors), Josephists, Lollards (English followers of John Wycliffe), Henricians and Esperonists, the Arnoldists, the Siccars, the Fratricellii (Little Brothers), Insabbathi (Sabbathless), Patarins (Sufferers), Passagenes (poor wanderers), Gazares, (Accursed and Abominable), Turil-upini (Dwellers with the Wolves), Albigenses (from the area of Albi), Toulousians (from Toulouse), Lombards (from Lombardy), Picards (from Picardy), Lyonists (from Lyons), There were also Catharists (Heretics), Publicans (compared to Roman sinners), Lollards, etc."[8]

Every dirty trick known to the satanically-inspired mind of man was used to discourage those who refused to practice infant baptism.

> "Among all the cruel bloodhounds, and persecutors of the Christians may well be counted Isdigerdis and his son, Geroranes, who not only flayed and roasted the Christians alive, but also

---

[7] *Martyrs Mirror* can be purchased at Rod and Staff Bookstore, Crockett, KY. 41413; and Amazon.com
[8] Ibid. 277.

split reeds, and bound them, with the cut side inwards, tightly around the naked bodies of the martyrs, whom they then drew out by force, thus shockingly lacerating the bodies of the Christians. They also confined the steadfast martyrs, naked, in cells, bound them hand and foot, and then chased in a great number of rats, which impelled by hunger, gnawed their bodies, and, in the course of time, entirely devoured them. Nevertheless, they could not, through these and similar cruelties, force many Christians to a denial of their Redeemer."[9]

In the year 1209, Pope Innocent III called for a crusade against the Waldenses in France. The Pope asked for volunteers against the unarmed, pacifist group of Christians who lived high up in the Alps. The Pope promised his church men forgiveness of sin and the spoils of war including taking over farms and fields as their own. As a result, tens of thousands of peasants took up arms hoping to gain wealth and lands. An estimated 200,000 Waldenses men, women and children were killed by the Pope's army in just a few months.

Two large cities, Beziers (Braziers) and Carcasone, were destroyed, together with many smaller towns and villages. They continued to attack them for the next 20 years and, "... in the city of Beziers alone about 60,000 men, women, and children were wiped out in one crusade."[10]

---

[9] Ibid.

[10] Broadbent, E. H. *The Pilgrim Church.* Grand Rapids, MI: Gospel Folio Press, 1999, 110, 111.

All told, millions were killed and made homeless over the centuries by the armies of the Roman Catholic church. These marauders forced believers to wander in the woods and mountains to escape their tormentors—all because they would not practice infant baptism and become members of the Catholic church. Christians were thrown from high cliffs, hanged, disemboweled, pierced through over and over again, drowned in lakes and rivers, torn by hungry dogs, burned alive at the stake, and even crucified.

In one case, 400 mothers high in the mountainous Alps of Italy fled from the approaching papal army and hid with their babies and toddlers in a cave in Castelluzzo, which was located 2,000 feet above the valley in which they lived. Upon discovery of their hiding place, the pope's men lit a large fire outside the cave entrance and women and children were all suffocated.[11]

The crusades sent against these people were similar to the crusades of tens of thousands of knights and foot soldiers sent to take Jerusalem back from the Muslims, only for these people it was because they had copies of the unadulterated Scriptures and because they would not practice the false doctrine of infant baptism.

Dave Hunt author of *A Woman Rides the Beast* wrote that, "Though no exact figures are available, the slaughter of Christians by the popes probably ran into the millions during the thousand years before the Reformation.[12]

---

[11] Orchard, G. H. *A Concise History of the Baptists*, 1855, 199.

[12] Hunt, D. *A Woman Rides the Beast.* Eugene, OR: Harvest House Publishers, 1994, 244.

13

BAPTISM & THE SPANISH INQUISITION

The Inquisition was another weapon that was originally put in place to be used against those who would not practice infant baptism; later it would also encompass the Jew and the Moor.

> "Making every allowance required by an historian and permitted to a Christian, we must rank the Inquisition, a ong with the wars and persecutions of our time, as among the darkest blots on the record of mankind, revealing ferocity unknown in any beast."[1]

Also, it is obvious that not every fact has been told in this book; it's an overview and not every martyr's story has been shared. However, one notable atrocity is the Spanish Inquisition. Even today, the Roman Catholic church retains the Inquisition, having changed its name to *The Sacred Congregation of the Holy Office.* The full story behind this barbaric arm of the Roman Catholic church becomes particularly important in light of the religious hatred that has resulted in global

---

[1] Hunt, D. *A Woman Rides the Beast.* Eugene, OR: Harvest House Publishers, 1994, 244.

terrorism fueled by the infamous Inquisition.

The Spanish Inquisition was formed in 1492 by the same King Ferdinand and Queen Isabella of Spain who commissioned a sailor named Christopher Columbus to seek a new route to spice-rich Asia. Ferdinand and Isabella, still referred to today as the *Reyes Catolicos* or Catholic Rulers, united Spain into one country by doing two things that year. (1) They were married and, (2) they expelled the Moors who were of the Islamic faith.

That is the well-advertised version of the story. But there is more. Forced baptism was one of the main issues. Before *los Reyes Catolicos,* the Iberian Peninsula was made up of various kingdoms, with Ferdinand and Isabella separately ruling over the largest two. As their collective moniker suggests, both of these rulers were staunchly of the Roman Catholic religion. They decided to marry, believing if they did they could meld their two large regions into one indomitable kingdom. Similar to Constantine's plan for Rome, they felt it was their religious duty or destiny (or both) to make their joint kingdoms into one bastion and put it under one religion. Of course, that religion would be Roman Catholicism.

Having completed the union, they set out to conquer other regions of Iberia in the name of Catholicism. At the time when these two monarchs and their kingdoms united, Spain was already a cultural center for the three major world religions that are monotheistic in nature—

Judaism, Islam and Christianity. All of these claim to have just one god/God as their head and Abraham as their spiritual patriarch.

It must be noted that, the term "catholic" means universal so that while the name, "the Roman Catholic church," boasts the title of church and encompasses all of the Roman Empire, there were in fact many groups of biblical believers throughout those countries who did not count themselves as Catholics.

These small churches considered infant baptism to be heresy and held tightly to the doctrines of the original New Testament Church. They closely followed the teachings of Jesus Christ and eschewed the traditions of man as taught by the Roman Catholic church, especially that of infant baptism.

Because the new rulers of the newly enlarged Spain felt their combined kingdoms (for they conquered other lands) should be thoroughly and particularly Catholic, they decided any other religions and non-Catholic sects would not to be tolerated and could not live within their borders. Any Roman Catholic could stay, of course. Everyone else must either convert to Roman Catholicism and be baptized into the church or leave—by choice or by force.

Thus Muslims and Jews and those Christians who would not practice infant baptism had to be baptized into Roman Catholicism, leave the country, or face death. This meant leaving behind homes, relatives, neighbors, money—virtually everything they had ever known. Given the option to stay or lose everything, many chose to stay and so went through the motions of becoming "Catholic," in name, if not in heart. Some packed up and left. Others took vows and were baptized into the Roman Catholic church which was the goal. The Catholic church knew what it had done. They knew those that remained behind did not have hearts converted to Catholicism. The diabolical Spanish Inquisition was set up to make sure those who had bowed their knee to Catholicism stayed true to the vows they had made under duress.

The mission of the Spanish Inquisition was "seek-and-destroy." Through a neighbor's tattletale or a child's inquiring teacher, victims were hunted down of all who, through their "conversion" had unwittingly brought themselves under the rule and punishments of the Roman Catholic church and the secular rulers who empowered her.

The Roman Catholic church assumed the label "Christian" but often it was in name only. The traditions of paganism that were prominent in the Roman Empire before Constantine's takeover of the church, had changed very little—although there was one exception. The Roman "church" now had installed Madonna as their queen of heaven, along with her little son.

Because the son carried the name of Jesus Christ, the Roman Catholic church could camouflage themselves as the embodiment of Christianity. With this camouflage, they were ready to track down and persecute the little groups of true believers who continued to rise up all over Christendom—popping up one group after another—bravely carrying the cross of Jesus Christ and following Book of Acts doctrine.

Within fifteenth century Spain, Book of Acts Christians was not the only group being persecuted. Judaism and Islam were also being persecuted. As two ethnically distinct groups of people, the Jews and the Moors, it was relatively easy to follow their fate because they were so distinctive from the "churched" population who were mostly whites. Here the distinctions ended.

Those Christians who would not practice infant baptism were subjected to the same horrors of rack and burning at the stake as the Jewish and Muslim population—only more so. In his book, *God, the Jews and History,* the Jewish author says that for every Jew killed by the Inquisitors, there were a thousand and one Christians that died at their hand.[2]

While the barbaric tortures and public murders experienced by the ancestors of the Jews and the Muslims have been kept alive in their descendant's hearts by the telling and retelling of the horrors, the followers of Christ have gone unnoticed and unmourned.

---

[2] Ibid., 256.

14

THE REFORMATION REVISITED

Martin Luther was just nine years old when the Spanish Inquisition began. As he grew up and became an adult, he looked around and saw the cruel persecution of people who refused to submit to the Roman Catholic church's traditions. He saw peasants sweating to earn enough money to support their families plus pay for indulgences to get dead family members out of a purgatory which he later learned was set in paganism—not the Bible.

Even as a monk, he did not have the privilege of reading the Bible for himself. He was terrified of dying. He said he knew that if he had died, he would have gone straight to hell. This is a strange confession coming from a man who had already been baptized as an infant and who would later teach and declare in the Augsburg Confession that "baptism saves."

When Luther became a professor of theology at Wittenberg University, he had access to a Bible and was able to seriously search the Scriptures as he hunted for God's plan of salvation. It was in the midnight hours as he searched the Bible, frantically seeking the way of salvation, that he came across a verse in the Book of Romans that stated, "The just shall live by faith."

> "For I am not ashamed of the gospel of Christ, for it is the power of God to salvation for everyone who believes, for the Jew first and also for the Greek. For in it the righteousness of God is revealed, from faith to faith; as it is written, *"The just shall live by faith...."*
> (Romans 1:16-17)

Suddenly, Luther understood! God gave him a revelation and he suddenly understood what the Scripture meant when it stated that it was faith in Jesus that would save his soul; that God had already provided atonement for his sin. Jesus had died and His blood had been shed in place of Luther having to pay the price at all. Luther's shame and penance meant nothing—Jesus' sinless blood had been substituted for his own sin-laden blood.

> "that if you confess with your mouth the Lord Jesus and believe in your heart that God has raised Him from the dead, you will be saved. For with the heart one believes to righteousness, and with the mouth confession is made to salvation."
> (Romans 10:9-10)

Suddenly Luther understood and humbly asked forgiveness and received it. Atonement had been accepted; eternal life had been granted. The peace of God filled Luther's heart. He had the experience that evangelicals (and Jesus) call "being born again."

> "Jesus answered and said to him, Most assuredly I say to you, unless one is born again, he cannot see the kingdom of God."
>
> (John 3: 3)

> "Jesus answered, "Most assuredly I say to you, unless one is born of water and the Spirit, he cannot enter the kingdom of God."
>
> (John 3: 5)

> "Do not marvel that I said to you, "You must be born again."
>
> (John 3:7)

Martin Luther—just like all evangelicals—began spreading the word. He told everyone he knew, including his Wittenberg students, that salvation was by faith alone with no works needed. Unlike most evangelicals, however, Luther was not rebaptized according to Bible standards.[1] Nevertheless, he began to write about his experience and others began circulating his letters without his permission. The Guttenberg press had recently been invented and the human mind was hungry for the written word.

So without Luther's permission, laypeople were reading everything he wrote. They were especially pleased because Luther's teachings were backed up with verses from the Bible—something hitherto forbidden the masses by the Catholic church. With the knowledge he had gained in searching the Bible to find the way of salvation, he was readily able to prove that the indulgence-selling

---

[1] Acts 2:38-39

Roman Catholic priests were fleeing their brothers and sisters in Christ—the very people they were supposed to be protecting.

Luther continued teaching his new revelation of salvation by faith alone, faith in the blood sacrifice on the cross and His resurrection from the dead. In Luther's Address to the Christian Nobility of the German Nation[2] he called for reform in the church. This was followed by more of his writings, all criticizing the pope and the Roman Catholic church.

The Roman Catholic church awoke to the possible damage to their reputation if this lowly monk continued exposing the lies and traditions that were extorting money from their people. They indignantly ordered that Luther's writings be burned. Luther, not to be outdone, brazenly burned theirs. Now the giant church was fully aroused. They angrily denounced his insubordination and demanded he present himself before them to recant.

The night before the Diet was to begin Luther arrived in the town of Worms, Germany. Along the way, multitudes had gathered in towns and waysides to wish him well. Once in Worms, he took lodging at an inn where people from all walks of life stopped by to thank him for setting them free and to give him a word of encouragement. This included barons, knights of the order,

---

[2] Ferm, Vergilius. *Classics of Protestantism* (New York: Philosophical Library, 1959. 51.

earls, priests, gentlemen, and "the commonality." All frequented his rooms until late the night before the Diet.[3]

The next day, Martin Luther was tried by a court that included high ecclesiastical officials. Although awed at first, he still refused to abandon his belief that salvation was by faith alone and not by works authorized by the church. This angered the gathering that was assembled against him and, as a result, Luther was excommunicated from the Roman Catholic Church. A ban was placed upon his life, which meant any one could kill him without fear of retribution.

Ordinarily, the government of the Roman Empire at the urging of the church would have burned Luther at the stake. But instead, for his own protection, he secretly entered into voluntary exile in a nearby abandoned castle. The world believed Martin Luther was dead.

The stay at Wartburg castle would last for ten long months. Martin Luther might not have known it, but he was at a crossroads. God wanted to use him to restore the church to its former purity. But principalities and powers wanted Martin Luther to take his hands off "their" church so that the devil could continue to rob pious people of their salvation.

Thus began the greatest spiritual battle of Luther's life. At the height of his career, Luther,

---

[3] Foxe, John. *Foxe's Books of Martyrs*. Springdale, PA: Whitaker House, 1981. 170.

used to being the center of attention, now found himself suddenly set aside. The battle he had fought so long and so well had suddenly defaulted to others among the Reform community.

Luther chafed at the boredom. Soon mental and physical problems evolved. It was in the midst of his torment that Luther said he fought enormous verbal battles with Satan and threw his famous inkpot at him. Luther's suffering was not unlike that of Job. The difference is that Job remained faithful to God during these times and Luther admitted that, in some of these trials and testing, he blasphemed God.

Whether Luther actually blasphemed God is not known, but true or not, after this time, there was a definite, downward, darkening spiral to his words and actions. Although he would still speak religious words, his beliefs and actions changed. It was at this time that he began to formulate a change in his doctrinal beliefs that would shut down the Reformation cold. He began to teach a different gospel than the gospel of faith in Christ's shed blood on the cross.

While in the castle, Luther was informed that some people were beginning to question infant baptism. They were insisting that infant baptism could not be found in the Bible. The townspeople and some of his old band of reformers were listening to three preachers from Zwickau who were teaching that infant baptism was a pagan doctrine and could not be found in the Bible. They were also teaching that it was heresy to say the gifts of the Holy Spirit had ceased. They said the Holy Spirit was needed to help and comfort the contemporary church as much as the early Church. They even suggested that speaking in tongues, as one part of the spiritual gifts, should be accepted. Many of Luther's old supporters were by now speaking in tongues themselves.

Philip Melanchthon was at first impressed by the three Zwickau prophets' "knowledge of the Bible, their belief that they were directly inspired by God, and their claim that they could prophesy by means of vision."[4] And he was not especially upset at the thought of allowing the gifts of the Holy Spirit to operate in the churches. In fact, some of Luther's supporters were already praying for the sick and using the prayer language of the Book of Acts Church. In fact, he rather liked the idea of having the same power that Jesus had displayed and that had been in evidence in the New Testament church.[5]

What Melanchthon was against, however, was that these same three prophets were also teaching that infant baptism could not be found in the Bible and were advocating for a return to biblical, Acts 2;38 water baptism. They insisted that infant baptism was not an authentic part of the new covenant. They pointed out some of Martin Luther's teaching and said that, had he still been alive, he would have agreed with them. And, in-

---

[4] Grimm, H. J. *The Reformation Era: 1500-1650.* New York: Macmillan, 1973. 123-24.
[5] Acts 2:3-10

deed, Martin Luther had written at the beginning of the Reformation that no Christian was saved by works of the Law (a ritual).

The idea that infant baptism might be removed from church doctrine greatly upset Philip Melanchthon. He sent an urgent message to the Wartburg castle, begging Luther to return to Wittenberg and sort this out. Melanchthon wrote that Luther was needed to determine the accuracy of some teaching that was taking place about infant baptism and the Holy Spirit.

As for Luther, he was tired of the solitude of the abandoned castle. He was only too happy to oblige. So when he arrived in Wittenberg, he was greeted like a war hero returned from the dead. He wasted no time listening to a doctrinal presentation from the three men.[6] Then, he quickly "sent the Zwickau prophets scurrying."

The simple country folk were overawed by Luther suddenly showing up. They marveled that he was not dead as they had feared because of the ban the Catholic church had placed on his head at the Diet of Worms. A ban meant that anyone, any place, could kill the Catholic's victim at will with no legal punishment. Now they looked to Martin Luther to sort out the issue over infant baptism.

As for Melanchthon, his part in all this was hardly complimentary. Because of his reliance

---

[6] Manns, P. *Martin Luther: An Illustrated Biography*. New York: Crossroad, 1982. 149.

upon Astrology—with its accompanying belief that "baptism saves" Melanchthon wanted Luther's presence in town. As for Martin Luther, he took the opportunity to side with Philip Melanchthon and assert his belief in infant baptism, leaving behind his God-given revelation that salvation is by faith alone.[7]

Martin Luther was glad to be back, asserting his influence as before. From the pulpit, he noted that the leader, Andreas Karlstadt, he had left in charge in his absence, had "gone over to the other side. " He preached eight sermons in a row and ridiculed Karlstadt from the pulpit because he had embraced the gifts of the Holy Spirit and believed He had a rightful position in the current church.

He now began to take the first of many open stands against the things of the Holy Spirit. This was in contrast to his pre-Reformation days; then he had written in complimentary terms regarding the Holy Spirit and the part He is supposed to play in the Church. But after he embraced infant baptism, Luther would change. He affirmed a belief in "cessationism," a theological word that meant he believed that the gifts of the Holy Spirit had ceased. He believed they had been given at the beginning of the church age, and now were

---

[7] "...that incurable follower of Astrology." (WAT 5 NO.5368, Summer 1540(K. Martin Luthers Werke: Kirtsche Gesamtausgabe. Tischreden, (Table Talk) Vols. 1-6 [Weimar, 1912-21]) (Luther by H. G. Haile, p215) (Luther by Heiko A. Oberman, p.330); Romans 1:17

no longer needed—albeit, he did not use Scripture to back up his assertion.

Sad to say, the things Luther said in his ridicule of the Holy Spirit at this time may possibly have been blasphemous.[8] If so, this would account for his accelerating aggravation toward those who embraced the Holy Spirit; and it would account for the downward spiral his life took from that point on. This observation is based on the Bible's statement that anyone who blasphemes the Holy Spirit will never be forgiven in this life or next.

> "Therefore I say to you, every sin and blasphemy will be forgiven men, but the blasphemy against the Spirit will not be forgiven men. Anyone who speaks a word against the Son of man, it will be forgiven him; but whoever speaks against the Holy Spirit, it will not be forgiven him, either in this age or in the age to come."
>
> (Matthew 12:31-32)

After Luther took his stand against the Holy Spirit and refused to consider the basis for the teaching of the men from Zwickau regarding infant baptism, he began trying to stop the reforms that were being carried out in certain of the churches in that area. These reforms were a direct result of Luther's past teaching against saint idolatry. Now, however, he tried to stop the zealous reformers from tearing down altars erected to

---

[8] Dyck, Cornelius J. *An Introduction to Mennonite History* (Scottsdale, PA: Herald Press, 1967), 23. J.M. Todd, *Luther: A Life* (New York, Crossroad, 1982), 290. Also Oberman, 198. Haile, 112–113, 116.

the saints. His excuse for his change of mind was that it was important to do reforms in a slow manner so the slowest among them could catch up with the new beliefs.

At the same time, Luther struck out against the peasants. He tried to hinder them from having free access to the Bible even though he had previously asserted that reading from the Bible was a primary right. So although Luther had previously championed Bible reading for the masses,[9] he now discovered the peasant's understanding of biblical truth could no longer be manipulated.

The peasants now had Bibles of their own to read which was due partly to Luther's own diligence in translating the Bible into the language of his fellow Germans during his exile at Wartburg castle. This meant they were taking note of things in the Roman Catholic church that did not line up with the Bible and were leaving the Catholic church. But, they were not joining Luther's new church either, as he had hoped. They were joining the little Anabaptist churches in the area.

These churches still preached a New Testament gospel as set forth in the Book of Acts. They did not preach an infant baptism which the peasants now knew—from their own Bible reading—could not be found in the Bible. Instead, they followed New Testament Book of Acts in-

---

[9] Simon, Edith. *Luther Alive: Martin Luther and the Making of the Reformation* (Garden City, NY: Doubleday, 1968), 302.

structions.[10] The pastor at one of these churches was Reverend Thomas Muntzer, a preacher Martin Luther had admired before Muntzer took him to task.

In fact, Muntzer and Luther originally felt a mutual affection toward each other. They admired each other's passionate evangelistic nature. They had once been in agreement in their assessment of the Roman Catholic Church. Both had stood up for what they believed to be the truth of the gospel, and both believed the Roman Catholic Church held doctrines that did not come out of the Bible but out of the Mystery Religions. They passionately denounced the popes and the heresy that emanated from their ungodly decrees. Muntzer, like Luther, was filled with anger against those who would hold back the truth of the gospel.

> "Then came the shameless woman with her red skirt, the spiller of blood, the Roman church, and broke with all other churches and declared that her ceremonies and gestures, patched together out of paganism, were the best and all others were an abominable atrocity.[11]

At first, Luther had agreed with Muntzer's bold analysis of the false doctrine in the church at Rome. Later, however, he changed his stance and turned against Muntzer. Luther had, perhaps un-

---

[10] Acts 2
[11] Mullet, Michael A. *Martin Luther* (New York: Taylor & Francis Group, 2004), 137–138. Brandt, ed., *Thomas Muntzer Sein Leben Und Seine* (1933), 136.

wittingly, returned to the Roman Catholic fold as he preached "baptism saves" and performed infant baptism in his church services. This meant Luther was espousing the very ritualism that had caught his ire in the first place.

By now, Martin Luther had led thousands of people out of the Catholic churches, believing that in doing so they were entering a church with true doctrine. Unfortunately, Luther himself was now deceived—for infant baptism does not save. Only faith in the blood of Christ saves. Yet nobody seemed to raise a hue and a cry, so trusting was the peasant population toward Luther at this time.

It is interesting to note that the apostle Paul wrote that if he had been willing to preach that the ritual of circumcision from the Old Testament was necessary for salvation under the new covenant, all persecution against him would have stopped. But Paul was not willing to compromise the gospel by preaching that a ritual of the law saves. He said, "And I, brethren, if I still preach circumcision, why do I still suffer persecution? Then the offense of the cross has ceased."[12]

The apostle Paul also had declared that if one believed a ritual was necessary for salvation, they would fall from grace.

> "Indeed I, Paul, say to you that if you become circumcised, Christ will profit you nothing. And I testify again to every man who becomes circum-

---

[12] Galatians 5:11

cised that he is a debtor to keep the whole law. You have become estranged from Christ, you who attempt to be justified by law; you have fallen from grace."

(Galatians 5:2-4)

After the Diet of Worms and his ten-month exile in Wartburg castle. Luther took a stand for infant baptism—thus negating his revelation that salvation is by faith alone. When he arrived home in Wittenberg, he took an open stand for "baptism saves" and reinforced his stand for infant baptism. When he did, the imperial ban that had been placed on his life that would usually result in death for the one banned, was never acted upon by the Catholic church. He was never arrested, tortured, or killed as was usual when an imperial ban was put on one's life. All persecution against him did stop. Luther would live out his life and finally die of natural causes.

Once one is aware of the part infant baptism has played in the death of Christians, it becomes easy to trace the truth of what happened to those who were falsely labeled heretics in the medieval church. When Martin Luther capitulated and began to teach the same doctrine of salvation that is taught by the Roman Catholic church—that of infant baptism—the Reformation lost its greatest champion for restoration of the true Gospel.

Up until then, Luther had been considered a friend of the peasant and so was very popular with them. So popular was he that he could have easily used his influence to bring the Church back to its New Testament purity. Instead, he stated that he believed in infant baptism with its corresponding belief that "baptism saves."

As a result of his flip-flop and return to the pagan belief that baptism—not Jesus Christ's finished work on the cross—saves, the great Reformation ground to a halt.

15

THE LUTHER NOBODY KNOWS

Shortly after the Diet of Worms, Luther and his reformers fell into disagreement and their coalition split apart. It was over infant baptism!

The Reformers who had stood together through thick-and-thin against the false doctrines and manmade-traditions of the Roman Catholic Church would now split-in-two over infant baptism. The part of the group that backed up Luther and Melanchthon, remained loyal to infant baptism and the belief that "baptism saves."

The other part of the Reform group rejected infant baptism and returned to New Testament instruction given by the Apostle Peter on the Day of Pentecost when the church began. They now sided with the persecuted Anabaptists who taught that salvation is by faith alone, followed by an after-conversion/full-immersion baptism.

> "Then Peter said to them, "Repent, and let every one of you be baptized in the name of Jesus Christ for the remission of sins; and you shall receive the gift of the Holy Spirit."
>
> (Acts 2:38)

This split amongst Luther's band of reformers never healed. Those who refused to any longer accept infant baptism now joined believers in the area who were being rebaptized upon faith and/or would not baptize their babies, believing infant baptism to be a false doctrine.

Almost immediately, great persecution fell upon those believers who had turned against infant baptism. The same kind of persecution that the Catholic church brought to bear against the Anabaptists (rebaptizers), Luther now also began to bring against them. This was not a new experience for the Anabaptists because, if the truth be known, this group was accustomed to being ridiculed and persecuted for their strong faith.[1] Because of the historical evidence recorded in the Martyr's Mirror, we know that there were large groups of Christians who stood against the false belief that "baptism saves" centuries before. So persecuting those who would not practice infant baptism was not a new idea thought up by Martin Luther.

With the loss of members of his reform group to the Anabaptists, Luther now began to persecute the Anabaptists in the same way as the Roman Catholic Church had been doing for centuries. The Catholics used laws of the state against "heretics" to keep from "getting their hands dirty. " This was possible because of an ancient law still

---

[1] van Braght, T. J. *Martyrs Mirror*. Scottsdale, PA: Herald Press, 1950. 198. [*Chron. Leonh, lib. 2. Will Baudart, Denckw., lib. 5. Hist. Joh. Wega, lib. 4, cap. 3. Theodoret., lib. 5, cap. 39.*]

on the books of the old Roman Empire—The Justinian Code.[2] For those who did not agree with the Catholic church, this law gave license to accuse them of heresy and then turn them over to the state as criminals for torture and execution if they would not recant their beliefs.

By 1530, Luther had begun to take advantage of an imperial edict that stated that all Anabaptists, whether men or women, were "to be destroyed with fire and the sword."[3] Thousands were imprisoned, tortured, and either burned at the stake or drowned. So great was Luther's vengeance toward the Anabaptists that he pursued them until every known Anabaptist was either dead or had fled.

> "Thus, during the second half of his life Luther found it quite in order that rebellious Anabaptists should be killed, and was capable of uttering ferociously unchristian words on the subject...Whereas earlier he had rejected the death penalty, he now approved a statement of Wittenberg theologians sanctioning executions."[4]

The Anabaptists were almost completely destroyed. Even five hundred years later, their descendants are few. Often living in seclusion even today, their small numbers tell the tale of murder

---

[2] www.christianitytoday.com/ch/131christians/rulers/justinian
[3] Smith, C. H. *Story of the Mennonites*. Newton, KS: Mennonite Publication Office, 1950. 29. (edict issued at the Diet of Speyer on April 23, 1529)
[4] Mjorud, Herbert. *What's Baptism All About?* (Carol Stream, IL: Creation House, 1978). 83.

that once ravaged their ancestors—fearful that persecution will once again pursue them should the Lutheran or Roman Catholic churches decide to renew their campaign against them. For even in this century, the Lutheran church continued to display its animosity in their statement of faith.[5]

Much has been written of Martin Luther's stand, Sola Scriptura. He has been considered a man of faith because of his insistence on Scripture as the base for all Lutheran doctrine. One look at the lack of scriptural evidence for infant baptism, however, and one must question that statement.[6] Even Luther's sola scriptura is under question because the actual context for that statement was his disparaging of the Holy Spirit whom Jesus sent to lead the Church in His absence. In his earlier years, Luther embraced the Holy Spirit. After he embraced infant baptism, he also vehemently opposed the work of the Holy Spirit. It would be said of him that his hatred of Spirit-filled believers almost outgrew his hatred of the pope and things Catholic.[7]

Old Luther also opposed the Jewish communi-

---

[5] Lohse, Bernhard. *Martin Luther: An Introduction to His Life and Work* (Philadelphia, PA: Fortress Press, 1986), 83.

[6] McClary, J. M. *The Secret About Infant Baptism That Everyone's Missing*. (Lake Mary, FL. Creation House. 2008.)

[7] Hostetler, John A. *Hutterite Society* (Baltimore, MD: John Hopkins University Press, 1974), 5. Hans A. Hillerbrand, *The Protestant Reformation* (New York: Harper Perennial, 1968), 214. Also Simon, 20–21, 340; Spitz, 97; Lohse, 77; Grimm, 219; Dyck, 6; Nigg, 303.

ty. Young Luther taught mercy toward the Jewish people and their plight. He was at first considered to be their friend because he preached understanding and friendliness toward them. Later he would change and show his Old Luther side. He began to speak hate-filled words toward them. [8]

This leads to another possible reason for the downward spiral that can be seen in Luther's life after he exited the Wartburg castle and returned to Wittenberg. The Bible speaks a curse against those who curse the Jews.

> "I will bless those who bless you, and I will curse him who curses you; and in you all the families of the earth shall be blessed."
> (Genesis 12:2)

Martin Luther's comments against the Jews became so hateful that many contemporary historians suggest that Hitler and his Third Reich took their license to commit atrocities against the Jews from Luther's sermons preached almost five hundred years earlier. He certainly affected those in his Lutheran denomination and rendered them paralyzed by his polemics and unable (or unwilling) to lend a hand to the Jews in their neediest hour.

In his book, *IBM and the Holocaust*, author Edwin Black further corroborates this rendition with his behind-the-scenes book written about Nazi Germany's rise to success using Luther's

---

[8] Friedenthal, Richard. *Luther: His Life and Times* (New York: Harcourt, Brace & Jovanovich, 1970), 303.

almost-forgotten words. It has been wondered by many just how Hitler was able to accomplish his nearly-impossible raid of Europe's Jewish population in so short a time period. Author Black wondered, too.

With the aid of nearly 100 volunteers, Black searched obscure Polish documents for clues into how Hitler so efficiently rounded up Jews and put them on trains to destruction in his concentration camps. By 1998, Black had ultimately assembled 20,000 pages of documentation from fifty archives, library manuscript collections, museum files and other repositories along with formerly classified government papers and obscure documents from European holdings that had never before been translated.[9]

It was discovered that a strategic alliance existed between Nazi Germany and America's then most powerful corporation, IBM, (known as National Cash Register Co.). It was through IBM's technology that Hitler was able to embark upon his dream of genocide for the Jews. Using IBM's advanced card system technology, forerunner of today's computers, a program was swiftly put in place that enabled the Third Reich to catalog, record and identify Jews through ancient church records, censuses, registrations, and other ancestral tracing documents.

With this information and sorting technology

---

[9] Black, Edwin. IBM and the Holocaust: The Strategic Alliance between Nazi Germany and America's Most Powerful Corporation. 2001. 13.

in place, Hitler and his men were able to facilitate the rounding up of the Jewish community by towns, automate its railroads, figure the amount of food needed to systematically starve Jewish laborers, organize concentration camp labor and keep accurate records of those daily being gassed in the ovens.[10]

Thus the following words of Martin Luther, spoken against the Jews, became prophetic as Adolph Hitler, with IBM's technological assistance, achieved the 6,000,000 deaths of the Holocaust.

> (a) "Luther dragged up all the ancient superstitions about Jews, dignifying them with his sanction. `They poison wells, steal Christian children whom they torture to obtain their blood.'"[11]
>
> (b) "In the first place, burn their synagogues. If Moses lived, he'd be the first to torch them. In the second place, tear down their houses, lest they teach at home. Also, take their books, forbid their rabbis to teach, deny them access to public highways...You shall not and cannot protect them unless you wish to partake of their abominations before God."[12]
>
> (c) "... let their usury be forbid them and all their gold and silver specie and treasure be seized and set aside. This being the cause; whatever they have is as stated above, stolen and robbed from

---

[10] Ibid. 115.
[11] Oberman, H. *Luther: A Man Between God and the Devil.* New Haven, CT: Yale University Press, 1989. 290.
[12] Ibid.

us by usury, for they no other living."[13]

(d) "... then we must take them out like mad dogs, lest we partake in their abominable blasphemy and vices, deserving God's wrath and being damned along with them. I have done my part. Let every man look to doing his. My hands are clean."[14]

Martin Luther also had a broad impact on his German contemporaries. His unfortunate handling of his followers among Germany's peasants was so devastating to a whole class of people that 100,000 deaths occurred during a few-day period of what came to be known as the "Peasants' War."

This happened in a way that only a few decades earlier would have been considered impossible. The peasants were his devoted friends and followers. They considered Luther to be one of them and were grateful that he had found the "faith alone" way of salvation. They appreciated that his expounding of Scripture had set them free from fear of death and the traditions of Catholicism. As a result, they were converting to a genuine relationship with Jesus Christ in record numbers.

With relief, they left behind the guilt and non-ending duties of Catholic membership, what with saying prayers for the dead, lighting candles, eking money together to pay to get their own sins

---

[13] Ibid.
[14] Ibid.

forgiven and masses said to aid their dead loved ones in Purgatory.

It was a loyal and grateful crowd that gave Luther their heartfelt thanks for his knowledge of the Bible that set them free. They were reading Scripture for themselves now—also thanks to Luther and his foresight in translating the Bible into the vernacular of the day. Now they could see for themselves that Purgatory was not in the Bible and the money they had been giving was, all along, going to aggrandize the Vatican, with a percentage to their local priest.

At that time, their trust in Luther knew no bounds. So they were shocked by his reaction to what they believed was a reasonable request of him to intercede for them with their landlords. They were working as near-slaves because of their rental agreements and they thought, what with Luther's considerable influence at that time, the landowners could be brought to the negotiating table and hear what they believed to be their just cause.

To their dismay and everlasting mistrust of him, Martin Luther sent a cruel letter to the landowners in which he sided with the peasant's wealthy antagonists and told them to take up arms against the defenseless peasants. They had asked that he intercede with their landowners asking for mercy and forbearance and a lifting of new taxes and unreasonably high rent.

Luther's letter to the landed gentry and armed knights encouraged physical assault against the unarmed farmers. In parrying for the favor of the wealthy land-owners, noblemen and knights, Luther denounced all peasants as rebellious, telling their landlords to "... stab and kill them [the peasants] like pigs."[15]

Knights and heavily-armed men were sent against the peasants' hoes and rocks. It escalated into a rampage that became known in history as the Peasant's War of 1525. Before the brief war ended, 100,000 peasants lay dead and the wealthy landowners had forever ruined the breadbasket of Europe. As for the peasants, the families of slain husbands and fathers were inconsolable; with Europe never fully recovering from the senseless loss of their former friends and neighbors.

The remaining peasants no longer trusted Luther; and to this day, historians shake their head over this loss of life and the part played in it by Martin Luther. As a result, Luther did not have enough followers left to set up his new church as he envisioned. So, an ambitious Martin Luther turned to the state government to do what he could not do in setting up his new religion.

A German language Bible had been produced by the Anabaptists for the purpose of distributing the accurate Scriptures to the population of Germany that their souls might be saved. It appeared in 1529, five years before the entire Lu-

---

[15] Grimm, H. J. *The Reformation Era: 1500-1650.* New York: Macmillan, 1973. 127–28.

ther Bible. It was called The Worms Bible after the name of the city in which it was published.[16]

The translation was by two Anabaptists, Ludwig Hetzer and Hans Denck. These men were accomplished scholars, thoroughly versed in Hebrew and Greek, as well as in Latin. Denck studied and received his Master's degree at the University of Basel, studying under and with the acclaimed Erasmus while Hetzer was an alumnus of both the University of Basel and the University of Paris.[17]

Approval of the Denck-Hetzer edition of the Bible was highly-acclaimed by scholar and layman alike. Within three years, thirteen editions had to be printed at Strasburg, Augsburg, Hagenau, and other places because all Germany was reading the Bible produced by the Anabaptists.[18] Eventually those who produced this Bible in the language of the German people were cruelly persecuted.

> "Denck, suffering with tuberculosis, under the decree of banishment and outlawry, died in hiding, in Basel, in 1529, a little before the Bible came from the press. Hetzer was arrested, condemned as a heretic, and beheaded the same year at Constance."[19]

Luther's Bible, meanwhile, was in process.

---

[16] Porter, John. *The World's Debt to the Baptists*, 1914, 138.
[17] Denck, Hans. *Ein Apostel der Wiedertaufer* by Ludwig Keller, p. 211; cited by Porter, 139.
[18] Ibid.
[19] Porter, John. *The World's Debt to the Baptists*, 1914, 139.

Every possible effort was then made to suppress the Anabaptist Bible. Printing offices, book shops where Bibles might be for sale, and private homes and individuals were searched in an attempt to destroy all copies. Today only three copies are known to be in existence and accessible to scholars. One copy is in the University of Bonn library; one is in a library in Stuttgart, and one is in the New York Public Library.

As for the peasants, as they discovered the truth, many left the infant baptism churches and joined the Anabaptists in the little house churches that Martin Luther and the Roman Catholic church were trying so hard to squelch.

16

BIRDS OF A FEATHER

Although Martin Luther has been given credit for the Reformation of the 1500's, most people are not nearly as aware that other reformers were also chipping away at the Roman Catholic stronghold in Europe. One of these reformers was Ulrich Zwingli of Switzerland.

Today members of the denominations that hearken back to Zwingli's legacy number more than 75 million and are in 107 countries. These include the Presbyterian church, the Reformed church, the Congregational church, and the Unity church.

More is known about John Calvin who came after him, than about Ulrich Zwingli who was born in Switzerland in January of 1484, two months after Luther was born. Zwingli was a highly educated man who studied in Basel and Bern, thriving centers of humanism. His studies took him to the University of Vienna where he became proficient in Greek and received a Master of Arts degree in 1506. Soon thereafter, he became a priest in the town of Glarus: "This combination of priestly duties with humanistic studies was exceptional, for records of the time show that many parish priests in Switzerland were ignorant, and that there were even some who had never read the entire New Testament."[1]

In 1518, Zwingli transferred to Zurich, Switzerland where he would have a significant impact. His biblical studies led him to reach the same conclusions in Switzerland as Martin Luther reached in Germany. He actually put many of his reforms into place before Luther.

However, the pathway Zwingli took to reach those conclusions was much different than the path Luther traveled. Luther anguished over his lost spiritual condition, doing penance and staying up all night mourning his sins.

Zwingli, on the other hand, and true to his humanistic education, did not agonize over his sins. He leaned toward an intellectual study of the Bible to achieve a form of peace with God. He, too, was concerned about the Roman Catholic church's exploitation of its members. This, and a strong bias against the conscription into military service required of Swiss men became burning issues for Zwingli.

Zwingli was working with reform in Zurich well before Luther nailed his "95 Theses" to the door of the Wittenberg church. Since Zwingli through

---

[1] Gonzales, Justo L. *The Story of Christianity, Vol.4. The Early Church to the Dawn of the Reformation.* HarperSanFrancisco-A Div. of HarperCollins Publishers. NY. 49.

his own studies came to almost the same conclusions as Luther had, his reform effort soon attempted to connect with Luther's effort in Germany but Luther was having none of it.

One thing both Zwingli and Luther (and later John Calvin) were in agreement about was infant baptism and the belief that "baptism saves" as applied to infant baptism.[2] As a result, both believed the society of their day was not in need of evangelization because of the laws that forced citizens to baptize infants as a means of "saving" them.

Meanwhile Conrad Grebel (1498-1526), Felix Manz, and George Cajacob were associated with Zwingli in the beginning of his work in Zurich. Unlike Zwingli, they would move away from Catholicism toward Protestantism. By the end of 1524, Grebel and Manz had taken a position against infant baptism. They wanted to establish a true church more like the New Testament model with only the two sacraments of believer baptism and the Lord's Supper.

On January 17, 1525, a debate between Zwingli and those who believed infant baptism was heresy took place in Zurich before the city council. The city council turned against those in favor of a return to New Testament baptism and they decreed that everyone under their jurisdiction must baptize their infants within eight days of

---

[2] Broadbent, E. H. *The Pilgrim Church*. Grand Rapids, MI: Gospel Folio Press, 1999. 163.

birth. Those who refused would be banished from Zurich.

Three days later, the city council issued another decree. This time they forbade opponents of infant baptism to meet together or to speak in public. Zwingli, who had once been an opponent of infant baptism himself, now went to battle against those who continued faithful to the book of Acts interpretation of the gospel.

Another thing that Martin Luther, Ulrich Zwingli and John Calvin all accepted, as did the Roman Catholic Church, was the Union between church and state. They believed violence was acceptable to use against "heretics", those who disagreed with them doctrinally. Thus the sword of the State became a tool to be used against all who had differing doctrinal positions. A year later, Ulrich Zwingli would be killed fighting against the Swiss Catholic army.[3]

Meanwhile, in 1511, one Michael Servetus was born in Villanueva, Spain. He was a Spanish physician and theologian whose beliefs led to his being burned at the stake by John Calvin. He had been living in Toulouse, France, where he studied law and became interested in the arguments for and against the doctrine of the Trinity.

In February 1530, he was invited by his patron/employer to attend the Emperor Charles V's coronation at Bologna. He was disgusted by the ostentation of the ceremony and the celebration

---

[3] http://www.newworldencyclopedia.org/entry/Ulrich_Zwingli

that accompanied the event. He left the gathering and proceeded to Geneva. There he came in contact with certain wellknown Reformation leaders and was able to discuss the Trinity with them.

He compared their ideas with the conclusions he had drawn and formulated his own opinion, noting that the Word is eternal and is God's self-expression and that the Holy Spirit is God's power going into the hearts of men.

To this, he added his conclusion that the Son is in essence a combination of God the eternal Word and mankind (the virgin shall bear a Son)—i.e., Christ. A triune God of Father, Son and Holy Spirit as three equal Gods in one seemed irreverent to him. He knew his simple description of the Godhead ascribed to the Trinity a different essence than at the Nicene Council and that this variance would bring both the Protestant church and the Catholic church against him.

Nonetheless, he wrote up his conclusion and sent his manuscript to John Calvin now leading the Reformation in Zurich, Switzerland. Calvin had been educated at the University of Paris, the University of Orleans, the College de Montaigu and the University of Bourges.

John Calvin had risen in importance at Zurich until he had more power than Zwingli ever had. Calvin wrote his most concise views on Christian theology in the Institutes of the Christian Religion.[4] The first edition in 1536 had only six chapters; the second edition in 1539 had 18 chapters because he added information from Philip Melanchthon's Loci Communes. In 1543, he again added to it, including a chapter on the Apostles' Creed.

Meanwhile, one thousand copies of Servetus' second manuscript were surreptitiously printed in Vienna in 1553. The manuscript, which he had labored over and wanted to get to John Calvin, discussed the relationship between the Holy Spirit and the born again experience of the Christian. (He is credited with using his discovery of pulmonary circulation of the blood to support the argument. Prior to knowledge of the content of Servetus' manuscript, it was inaccurately taught by the medical profession.)

Servetus' groundbreaking (and unwelcome) argument was that both God the Father and Christ his Son were dishonored by the emperor Constantine at the Nicene Council. He felt the Trinity implicit in the Nicene Creed did not honor God and did disservice to the redemptive role Christ fulfilled in bring salvation to the world. In fact, Servetus was so bold as to openly state he felt the doctrine of the Trinity, as stated at the Nicene Council, brought about the downfall of the New Testament church.

It was Michael Servetus' opinion that the way

---

[4] *Hesselink, I. John (2004), "Calvin's theology", in McKim, Donald K., The Cambridge Companion to John Calvin, Cambridge: Cambridge University Press, pp. 74–75.*

to restore the church was to separate it from the government and use only "those theological formulations" as could be proved from the Bible and that were approved prior to the Nicene Council by the pre-Constantinian fathers.

When some of the letters that Servetus had written to Calvin fell into the hands of de Trie, a former citizen of Lyon, he reported Servetus to the Inquisitor General at Lyon. Servetus was seized and imprisoned. Lax security allowed him to escape before his trial and he headed for Switzerland. Not to be outdone, the Catholic church made a life-size image of his body and burned him in effigy.

To the surprise of many, Dr. Michael Servetus showed up in Geneva at one of John Calvin's meetings, perhaps hoping for one more opportunity to dialogue with him. However, he was recognized in the audience. Police arrested him and he was tried for the heresy of disbelief in the Trinity and infant baptism.

Servetus' Geneva trial lasted for more than two months. Calvin was prominent as his accuser. As he had promised earlier, if Servetus was caught on his turf, he would never leave alive. He proposed execution by beheading but when urged to have him put to death by burning at the stake, he reluctantly complied.

On October 27, 1553, Servetus was taken to the edge of Champl with the townsfolk gathered around. He was chained to a stake, a sulphurous wreath set on his head and green wood piled high around him.

Because the wood was wet, it took many tries to light a tenuous fire. It burned slowly, crackling and spitting. The wreath was lit. It sparkled momentarily, burning his eyes and ears and, after consuming his beard, fell to the ground.

Servetus refused to recant and after thirty minutes, his cries of pain were heard no more. The slow-burning wood had done its job. One thing his death did was to bring an end to the controversy brought on by Gregory of Naazanius' insertion of a Trinity at the Nicene Council.

The final edition of Calvin's Institutes came out in 1559—six years after Michael Servetus was burned at the stake. By then, The Institutes was eighty chapters in four volumes with each book named after a statement from the Nicene Creed.[5] His theology expanded on his favorite subjects but changed little from his youth to his death and is still thoroughly studied in seminaries that feed the Reform churches.

Meanwhile, the thirty years war continued. The Lutherans and the Reformed churches were against each other and both were against the Catholics and all the religions were against those who would not practice infant baptism. As a result, the peasants were now in a worse predicament than before Martin Luther ever set out to reform the Church!

> "For more than twelve centuries, baptism in the way taught and described in the New Testament

---

[5] Ibid. https://en.wikipedia.org/wiki/John_Calvin_bibliography

had been made an offense against the law, punishable by death."[5]

All the infant baptism churches—whether Roman Catholic, Lutheran or Reformed—now began to freely use the state's tools of torture and death as they vied for power over the laypeople of the land. Seventy years after Luther's death, the battle still raged.

In 1616 A.D., the followers of Martin Luther, Ulrich Zwingli and John Calvin (calling themselves respectively the Strict Lutherans, the Zwinglians and the Calvinists) were not being successful in ridding their lands of those who would not practice infant baptism.

It was decided that there needed to be a "final solution" to the Anabaptist problem. They invited the Protestant infant baptism churches to the Netherlands where a Synod of Dort had been called. The decision was reached that these various Protestant groups were to stop persecuting each other. They could focus all their attention on getting rid of the little house churches who were continuing to go on with their lives evangelizing and baptizing new converts.

> The Synod of Dort "was the greatest synod of Reformed churches ever held. Present were delegates not only from the Reformed churches in the Netherlands, but also from the Reformed churches in England; in the Palatinate, Hesse, and Bremen in Germany; and in Switzerland.

---

[6] Ibid. 172.

> Delegates from France and other parts of Germany had also been invited but were unable to attend."[7]

The Synod of Dort unanimously condemned the Anabaptist teachings. They wanted only infant baptism rather than a water baptism that followed repentance.[8] These Protestant churches decreed death for those who did not practice infant baptism and/or were rebaptized. They used the old Justinian Code to carry out their goal.

Thus the Protestants joined with the Roman Catholic Church who for centuries had been burning at the stake those who would not practice infant baptism.

> "For a hundred years, the slaughter of innocents would continue. The Roman Catholic Church, the Lutheran church and the Reformed churches all participated and gave their full assistance and assent—all because they would not practice infant baptism. There was not a safe place in all of Switzerland or in South Germany, Austria, and Moravia. All up and down the Rhine River and the upper Danube, Anabaptists were being slaughtered for their faith." [9]

> "For a full century and more, not only in Switzerland, but all over, south Germany, Austria, and Moravia, up and down the Rhine and the

---

[7] spurgeon.org/~phil/creeds/dort.htm
en.wikipedia.org/wiki/Synod_of_Dort
[8] Acts 2:38, 39
[9] Smith, C. H. *Story of the Mennonites*. Newton, KS: Mennonite Publication Office, 1950. 10.

upper Danube, where they were found, Anabaptists had to pay the extreme price for their faith…to all this terrible butchery the churches whether Catholic, Lutheran or Reformed, gave their full assent and assistance."[10]

The smaller churches, scattered as they were, were effectively crushed, except for a remnant hidden away in the wilderness.[11]

---

[10] Nigg, Walter. *The Heretics.* (Dorset Publishing, NY. 1990.) 304.

[11] Broadbent, E. H. *The Pilgrim Church.* Grand Rapids, MI: Gospel Folio Press, 1999. Also Gonzalez; Kuiper. www.christianchronicler.com/history1/zwinglian_revolt.html

17

ANCIENT CHURCH IN THE ALPS

> "Avenge, O Lord, thy slaughtered saints whose bones lie scattered on the Alpine mountains cold: Even them, who kept thy truth so pure of old, when all our fathers worshiped stocks and stones, forget not; in thy book record their groans..."
>
> (Milton, Paradise Lost)

There is an amazing story that must be told. The reason the true Church is beginning to flourish again is that, in the early centuries, God hid a remnant of the Book of Acts Church high in a place of safety in the northern Alps.

They were a stalwart group of Christians who could be trusted to keep the light of the Gospel burning brightly down through the long dark centuries of persecution that lay ahead for those declared heretics by the false church!

This group, known to the outside world as "the Waldenses," piously kept the instructions handed down to the apostles on the Day of Pentecost when the Holy Spirit was sent and the Church age began (see Acts 2). They kept Christ's teachings alive through more than twelve long centuries, despite the cruelest torture and persecution. Relief would not reach them until 1870 A.D.

In the early centuries, the Waldenses had escaped Rome's corrupting of all things holy. They quietly left Rome and entered a place God prepared for them beforehand—a place almost inaccessible with tall cliffs and raging rivers and narrow snow-covered passes and fruit trees and sun-drenched meadows.

It was a place where worship could be conducted according to the dictates of their Saviour, Jesus Christ and families could be raised in peaceful surroundings. It was to this group that Jesus referred in His prophetic warning of coming apostasy:

> "Now when the dragon (Satan) saw that he had been cast to the earth, he persecuted the woman (God's people) who gave birth to the male *Child* (Jesus). But the woman was given two wings of a great eagle, that she might fly into the wilderness to her place, ...
> (Revelation 12:13-14, clarification added)

With faith in their hearts and accurate copies of the unadulterated Scriptures in their possession, the Waldenses refused to bow their knee to the Roman Catholic church. Armies were sent against them in an attempt to force them into submission. They continued to follow New Testament practices as found in the Book of Acts; and they continued to embrace the Old Testament as well as the New.

As a result, the Roman Catholic church spent centuries trying to break their spirit and get them to apostatize. The Waldenses were considered a particular enemy to Catholic teachings and could not be persuaded to turn their back on the Apostle Peter's teachings in the Book of Acts.[1]

In some situations, the Roman Catholic church would send a lone priest or a papal army up into the northern Alps to seize and slaughter the Waldensians —or perhaps capture a child to raise as a Catholic. A lone woman picking berries might have her tongue cut out for confessing Christ.[2] Other times, papal troops descended on a village or town in the middle of the night and the inhabitants were slain and their property confiscated.

Any caught sharing the gospel and baptizing the resulting new convert were tortured and burned at the stake; sometimes mutilation and other obscene torments took place first. But they would not deny their Saviour. John Milton would write his famous Paradise Lost about the terror brought down upon this simple people as they kept the faith and shared the light of the Holy Scriptures with those kept captive in Rome's false church. Today we can only guess the number of precious souls rescued from the gates of hell by the Waldenses' simple technique of disguising themselves as peddlers and distributing hand-

---

[1] Acts chapter 2 and 15
[2] Wylie., J. A. The History of the Waldenses, 1860. 69-70.

written Scriptures in the valleys below.

During those years, the Waldenses raised their children amongst beautiful scenery and taught them to reverence God and not fear a martyr's death. Chosen pastors called barbes made dangerous forays down into the Piedmont valleys below to bring the Gospel to those who showed an interest in hearing the truth. The Waldenses remained concerned lest those under the control of the Roman church might die without ever hearing the Gospel preached. The compassionate Waldenses gave their very lives to pay that huge price for sharing the one and only true Gospel that alone would save eternal souls from Hell's fire.

Down through the ages, this small remnant of devout believers kept the light of the Gospel burning through centuries of hardship and torture. It is not so surprising that this group survived, for God had His hand upon them; what is surprising, is that their faithfulness is not remarked upon every time we gather together as a church. Unknown and unsung, the Waldenses stayed at their post until the baton could be passed and an unadulterated copy of the Scriptures turned over to representatives of the great Reformation.

The Waldenses were a small group of Anabaptist that escaped the clutches of the Roman Empire in the early centuries after Rome's takeover of the church at Rome. An estimated time for this was the early centuries and probably can be traced back with some accuracy to the time of the Bracerensian Council's decree, in 610 A.D., that all must practice infant baptism or die. According to van Braght's Martyr's Mirror, it was known as the bloody edict.

If that date is the actual date, then there is another amazing Scripture that prophesied the event. Not only did it concisely report the Jews' travail as they carried the seed that would put a Savior on this earth, but it foretells Satan's preoccupation with awaiting that Seed to kill it before God's purposes succeeded.

It also tells the story of Jesus' ascension back into heaven and the need for His followers to flee into the wilderness to preserve the Word of God. Read it with great interest for it tells a tale that, again, shows that God is sovereign. Read it and be amazed that this remnant of the Church was able to confound the "mother of harlots" that rode the "scarlet beast" that was covered with words of blasphemy.

It was undoubtedly this remnant who would venture down into the valleys with their precious pieces of Scripture and evangelize the peasants of those centuries—to the chagrin of the infant baptism churches.

> "Then I witnessed in heaven an event of great significance. I saw a woman clothed with the sun, with the moon beneath her feet, and a crown of twelve stars on her head. She was pregnant, and she cried out because of her labor pains and the agony of giving birth. Then I wit-

nessed in heaven another significant event. I saw a large red dragon with seven heads and ten horns, with seven crowns on his heads. His tail swept away one-third of the stars in the sky, and he threw them to the earth. He stood in front of the woman as she was about to give birth, ready to devour her baby as soon as it was born. She gave birth to a son who was to rule all nations with an iron rod. And her child was snatched away from the dragon and was caught up to God and to his throne. And the woman fled into the wilderness, where God had prepared a place to care for her for 1,260 days."

(Revelation 12:1-6 NLT)

It is likely this group, more than any other, was ordained of God to be responsible for keeping alive the Gospel down through the long, tumultuous dark ages. The last verse is of especial great interest to us because it tells how long they would be exiled in the wilderness. It was for a specified time—1,260 days.

Is it not possible that the 1,260 days of persecution mentioned in the above Scripture might camouflage the 1,260 years of persecution that came against the Waldenses as they were pursued by the evil Roman Empire –alias- the Church of Rome—in an effort to annihilate their witness? This faithful remnant persevered until 1870 when France's armies were finally forced to leave them alone and return home because they had been defeated in their war with Germany.[3]

---

[3] Ibid. 203.

If one counts the years between "the bloody edict" of 610 A.D. to the signing of a peace treaty, the Statuo of Carlo Alberto which promised Italy's citizens freedom to choose whom they would worship in 1848 A.D. (but which was not put into effect until 1870 A.D.), one finds that 1,260 years have elapsed.

During that time, numerous crusades were sent against them. For example, in 1487 Pope Innocent VIII called for a crusade against the Waldenses in Italy, Germany, and elsewhere. He promised forgiveness of sins and a share in the plunder to those who joined. Charles VIII of France and Charles II of Savoy agreed to raise an army for the destruction of the Waldenses.

This regular army numbered about 18,000 soldiers and thousands of "ruffians" joined, urged on by the promise of forgiveness of sins and the expectation of obtaining spoil from the Waldensian possessions. Wylie describes these volunteers as "ambitious fanatics, reckless pillagers, and merciless assassins."

> "The Waldenses were burned; they were cast into damp and horrid dungeons; they were smothered in crowds in mountain caverns, mothers and babes, and old men and women together; they were sent out into exile in the winter night, unclothed and unfed, to climb the snowy mountains; they were hurled over the rocks; their houses and lands were taken from them... Thousands of heretics" or Waldenses, "old men, women and children, were hung, quartered, broken upon the wheel, or burned alive and

their property confiscated for the benefit of the king, and Holy See."[4]

Thousands of Bible-believing Christians perished. Entire villages became burned out shells. Women were raped and viciously murdered; children were dashed against trees and thrown off cliffs; homes and crops destroyed.

More than 3,000 Waldensian Christians, men, women, and children, perished in a single incident when the entrance to a cave called Aigue-Froid where they had fled for safety was stopped up and set afire. Their property was then given to the ragtag army of dissidents that made up the papal crusade. Entire valleys were burned and pillaged, populations murdered. One crusade against the Waldensians lasted for an entire year before all inhabitants succumbed.[5]

The Waldenses today stand victoriously before God in heaven having remained faithful to the gospel amidst horrendous assaults upon their people for sharing the gospel, never betraying the name of Jesus Christ. The suffering recorded by their grieving brethren in the Martyrs Mirror showed torture and deception devised by a satanic mind. For surely another human being would never do the things to a fellow human being that were done to them.

> .... no town in Piedmont, under a Vaudois pastor, where some of our brethren have not been put

---

[4] Ibid. 29. (*Thompson - The Papacy and the Civil Power*)
[5] Schaff, Philip. *History of the Christian Church*, V, 519.

to death...Hugo Chiamps, of Finestrelle, had his entrails torn from his living body, at Turn. Peter Geymarali, of Bobbio, in like manner had his entrails taken out at Lucerna, and a firerce cat thrust in their place to torture him further...James Baridari perished covered with sulphurous matches, which had been forced into his flesh under the nails, between the fingers, in the nostrils, in the lips, and over all his body, and then lighted. Daniel Revelli had his mouth filled with gunpowder which being lighted, blew his head to pieces. Maria Monnen, taken at Liousa, had the flesh cut from her cheek and chin bone, so that her jaw was left bare, and she was thus left to perish....[6]

Entire armies were sent to destroy the Waldenses in the 17th century. The Inquisition's intent was not only to kill whole families but to destroy their literature and Scriptures as well. In their forays into the difficult mountainous terrain, priests accompanied the papal armies to make certain of this. Hearing of the devastation repeatedly sent against the Waldenses Oliver Cromwell, as representative of England's ruler, attempted to intervene in their tragedy.

By that time, practically all of their documents had been destroyed but Cromwell sent as his representative, a Mr. Samuel Morland, into northern Italy to gather up any remaining materials he could find that would authenticate their beliefs. In 1658, he sent their remaining litera-

---

[6] Wylie, J. A. The History of the Waldenses, 1860. 69-70.

ture back to England to be deposited in the University of Cambridge library where they are still available as the Morland Collections.

The Morland F packet, in particular, is of interest to us. It contains manuscripts from the 14th century that contain the entire New Testament and parts of the Old, as well as the apocryphal writings *"in the Peidemontese dialect of Provencal or Occitan."*[7]

Nevertheless, persecution would continue for two hundred more years. It would not be until 1870 that the Waldenses would at last be free of the cruel attacks of the Roman Catholic church. During those long ugly years of persecution, one Pope more than any other—if only because of the thirty-two year duration of his reign—would be responsible for the deaths and property destruction of the Waldenses. His name was Pope Pius IX who reigned from 1846 to 1878.

During his pontificate he convened the First Vatican Council (1869-70) which decreed papal infallibility and defined the dogma of the Immaculate Conception of the Virgin Mary. He was the last pope to rule as Sovereign over the Papal States. It was in the year 1870 that the Papal States fell to King Victor Emmanuel II and his Italian Army and they were incorporated into the Kingdom of Italy.

The Italian Army's control of Italy meant that

---

[7] www.wayoflife.org/files/4ef3f30d5ea4253059dc014c8c9f6db3-79.html

both the Jews and the Waldenses no longer had to cope with the Roman Catholic church or fear the Pope. The fact that both were set free from papal control in the year 1870 is curious. Also curious, is the papal decree sent out in 610 A.D. by the Roman Catholic church ordering that any caught making new converts and baptizing them according to Peter's instructions given on the Day of Pentecost were to be killed.

> ...Wherefore in 610 A.D., in the Second Bracerensian Council, among other articles, it was established, decreed, and published; "That infants must be baptized, as necessary to their salvation." *(Seb. Franck, Chron., Rom., Kett., fol.74, col.2. P.J. Twisick, Chron., 7th book page 213, col.2)*[8]

A closer examination and one notes that 1,260 years have passed between 610 and 1870. Is this important? In the following verse, this same number of days are mentioned as the length of time that God would feed (care for) a remnant of His people. With God, a day is as a thousand years and a thousand years is as one day. Dare we wonder if "1,260 days" is poetic language for 1,260 years?

> Then the woman fled into the wilderness where she has a place prepared by God that they should feed her there one thousand two hundred and threescore days.
>
> (Revelation 12:6)

---

[8] van Braght, T. J. *Martyrs Mirror*. Scottsdale, PA: Herald Press, 1950. 214.

Are not the Waldenses who protected the gospel and evangelized their neighbors in the valleys below for 1,260 years, "the woman who fled into the wilderness," for whom God prepared a place of refuge? And, indeed, are not the northern Alps with its rugged cliffs and raging rivers "the earth" that provided protection for them? With faith in their heart and God on their side, they weathered the storm that came against them from the Pope's men for 1,260 years.

> But the woman was given two wings of a great eagle that she might fly into the wilderness to her place, where she is nourished for a time and times and half a time, from the presence of the serpent.
> (Revelation 12:14)

> But the earth helped the woman (*the mountainous landscape*), and the earth opened its mouth (Waldenses witness) and swallowed up the flood which the dragon had spewed out of his mouth.
> (Revelation 12:16, emphases added)

Ah, but there is more! In between the above two verses is another verse that is of ultimate importance! Not only is the story accurately told in the 12th chapter of Revelation about a remnant of God's people fleeing into the wilderness, it warns of the weapon the serpent would bring against the Church in his attempt to destroy it—it would be a false water baptism! This is the secret that everyone's missing!

> So the serpent spewed water out of his mouth (it was from his lips that the lie about a false water

> baptism would come) like a flood after the woman (a woman always stands for God's church), that he might cause her to be carried away (destroyed) by the flood.
> (Revelation 12:15, emphases added)

So then, is the 1870 A.D. date, a date when both the Jewish community and the Waldenses were set free from the Roman Catholic church, meant to convey a special meaning to us?

> And I will give power to my two witnesses, and they will prophesy one thousand two hundred and sixty days, clothed in sackcloth.
> (Revelation 11:3)

Are not these two—the Jew and the Christian—also God's two witnesses spoken of in the Book of Revelations?

18

INQUISITION ENTERS COLONIAL SHORES

It was 1565, nine years after the death of Martin Luther. On colonial shores, French Protestants called Huguenots had just been murdered by the Inquisition of the Roman Catholic church after making a dangerous journey to what is today known as St. Augustine, Florida. They had hoped to leave behind the religious persecution happening all over Europe at the hands of the Roman Catholic church.

After a long sea voyage, they landed in Florida and founded a small colony suitable to raise a family and worship God in what is today the idyllic city of St. Augustine, Florida.

Peace was short-lived. Persecution like that in the old Roman Empire was already raising its itchy fingers into the new world. News reached the court of King Phillip II of Spain that Protestants had settled in an area assigned to him by the Roman Catholic church. He dispatched eleven ships and 1,000 troops to deal with the interlopers. As they neared the Florida coastline, several ships were destroyed by bad weather, the remaining vessels continued on.

Completely unaware of the impending danger, the entire Huguenot colony was wiped out. In the end, two hundred fifty-three men, women, children and infants, lay dead before the dreaded *Spanish Inquisition* finished their task, raised anchor, and set sail for home.

In 1607, the new Jamestown Expedition beached on colonial shores. This new group was under the crown of England and not such easy prey as the unprotected group that had been martyred forty years earlier. This is the well-advertised account of the Jamestown Expedition. However, there is much more!

Something unusual occurred in the very beginning days of the expedition's arrival on New England shores that would forever change the history of the world, and certainly that of the United States of America!

Three days after the expedition's arrival, while the captain and leaders onboard were discussing rules governing their undertaking, something happened in which God had a hand. Aboard that ship was a chaplain who had undertaken this hazardous journey for a different reason than most of the ship's crew.

He brought with him a few hand-picked men who were equally keen as he was in claiming the new land in the name of Jesus. Before the rest of the crew set foot on what would be named Cape Henry, Chaplain Robert Hunt led a few men ashore, bearing with him a large wooden cross.

Their purpose was to put a stake in the ground

and proclaim the name of Jesus Christ over the land. Their intent was to be able to practice Christianity according to biblical principles. For that purpose, Rev. Hunt brought with him from England the oaken cross that would claim colonial shores in honor of their Lord and Savior. To this end, he embarked three days earlier than the rest of the ship's crew so that he and his comrades would be first to dedicate the land to God.

They held a short ceremony of prayer, committing the land to God's purposes in bringing them to the shores of this wild river. Their expressly stated desire was to "properly baptize!" They wanted biblical Christian baptism to be practiced. This information was uncovered just thirty years ago when, on a hunch, a worker from the Christian Broadcasting Network went to visit a small library in Portsmouth, Va. near where the ship's occupants had come ashore.

There she thumbed through a 700-page volume at the Portsmouth Public Library that revealed the long lost reason for the Jamestown expedition. In an April/1980 edition of Flame, a Christian Broadcasting Network publication, she uncovered the main reason these men had left England—it was to convert new souls and disciple converts according to instructions found in the Bible.

> "... First to preach and baptize into Christian religion, and propagation of the Gospel, to recover out of the arms of the devil, a number of poor and miserable souls...."[1]

---

[1] *Flame.* CBN. April, 1980.

The long arm of the Inquisition had been felt all throughout the known world. Torture and death was being felt worldwide if one remained faithful to the instructions given by the Apostle Peter on the Day of Pentecost

> "Peter said to them, "Repent, and be baptized every one of you in the name of Jesus Christ so that your sins may be forgiven; and you will receive the gift of the Holy Spirit...."
>
> (Acts 2:38-39)

Burning at the stake or death by the rack followed anyone who stayed true to the New Testament teachings of Jesus Christ. God had heard the prayers of those tortured for their faith and was turning things around and opening up a whole new world that He had kept in reserve. The Gospel would soon go forth freely. But, for a time, the faithful would need to continue to stand.

The Puritans and the Separtists, both of old England, were being persecuted by their nations' corrupt Anglican church. They believed the church's ecclesiastical courts were corrupt, their bishops lived licentious lifestyles and their liturgy was too Catholic. The Puritans complained to the leadership but that was of no avail because the church was an arm of the state. Their complaints made them enemies of the government.

The Separtists, on the other hand, refused to be part of a church filled with corruption. They left the mother church and formed their own societies. That did not please the king either and both groups were forced to flee England for their lives' sake.[2]

In 1630 the Puritans arrived in New England (the Pilgrims arrived in 1620). They established the Massachusetts Bay Colony and began church services. As soon as they were safely ensconced in the New World, they turned and began persecuting the Separtists (Baptists), who had also fled England. The reason the Puritans persecuted the Separtists? They would not practice infant baptism! Old world practices were attempting to surface in the colonies!

A year later, Roger Williams, a Baptist preacher, arrived. He and his wife Mary were at first welcomed by the Puritans until they realized that Williams believed infant baptism to be heresy and, when he immediately began converting the Native Americans, he baptized them according to biblical standards. He was also against setting up a State church which had proved so disastrous to believers in Europe.

When Puritans learned this, they passed an ordinance that outlawed Williams' preaching.[3] Five years later, in 1635, he got wind of the fact that he was about to be seized and sent back to England to be put to death. Rather than die a martyr's death, Williams escaped and joined the Native Americans whom he was already evangelizing. Meanwhile, he had the God-given good

---

[2] www.mainstreambaptists.org/mbn1/english_separatists.htm
[3] www.britannica.com/EBchecked/topic/644376/Roger-Williams

sense to apply for a special charter from the English Parliament for those *distressed of conscience* for faith's sake.

Likewise, in 1638 Anne Hutchinson, mother of fourteen, was condemned as a heretic by the Puritan church because she was questioning infant baptism.[4] She was forced out of the colony and had to flee, along with her husband and children, to Providence, Rhode Island. There she suffered a miscarriage. In the midst of the trauma, rumor circulated that the fetus she was carrying was conceived by the devil.

Her Quaker friend Mary Dyer was hanged by her neck for the same sin of questioning infant baptism.[5] After her husband's death, Anne and all but one of her children were massacred by Indians in the wilderness.

Persecution of those who would not practice infant baptism was escalating. It was the first and unexpected indication that things were taking a bad turn in the New England colonies, similar to what had been happening (and would continue to happen for two more centuries) in the old Roman Empire.

Finally, on March 14, 1644, Roger Williams received the sought-after charter from the English Parliament! It gave him permission to establish a colony in Providence, Rhode Island as a *"shelter for persons distressed for conscience."*

---

[4] www.britannica.com/EBchecked/topic/277653/Anne-Hutchinson
[5] www.britannica.com/EBchecked/topic/175035/Mary-Barrett-Dyer

19

SEPARATION OF CHURCH & STATE

An attempt to silence the preaching of the true Gospel was once again in progress—this time in the new world. Believers who came to the New England colonies with a desire to share salvation with their friends and neighbors, as well as the Native Americans, were soon being harassed and imprisoned. They were accused of preaching or teaching in private homes.

This preaching infuriated those churches that wanted to limit teaching to what was being taught in the Anglican church with its emphasis on infant baptism. One example of the growing violence against those who were preaching the New Testament instructions given by Apostle Peter happened in Fredericksburg, Virginia.

The Spotsylvania sheriff and his deputies surrounded five Baptist preachers on June 4, 1768. Seizing them, they brought them before the court at Fredericksburg, Virginia. They were charged with disturbing the peace and bail was set. The charge? The preachers were "in the habit of running into private homes and making discussions."[1]

---

[1] Ibid.

Three years later, Mr. Morgan Edwards of Crozer Theological Seminary in Pennsylvania visited Virginia in 1771. There, he told about a certain Elijah Craig who had charges made against him for illegal preaching. Mr. Craig was one who had been put in "gaol" at Orange for testifying about what Jesus had done for him. He was held in an inner dungeon and fed a ration of daily bread and water through an opening in the door.

He was held for a lengthy period but used his time preaching through the bars to other prisoners which caused him to be isolated even further. This was because the thirteen American colonies were beginning to officially recognize "established" state churches just like in the old country.

By the beginning of the Revolutionary War, nine of the colonies already had state religions set up that favored only infant baptism churches. Among the colonies, only Rhode Island permitted complete freedom of worship, a legacy of Roger Williams and his Baptist followers. The Congregational church was the state religion of Connecticut, Massachusetts and New Hampshire; the Episcopal Church was, more or less established by law, in six colonies: New York, Maryland, Virginia, North Caroline, South Carolina and Georgia. Three colonies, Pennsylvania, Delaware and New Jersey, had no established religion.[2] Among the colonies, only Rhode Island permitted com-

---

[2] Armstrong and Armstrong. 95.

plete freedom of worship, a legacy of Roger Williams and his Baptist followers.

The murdering of more than 50 million people had occurred overseas because the Roman Catholic church (and later, Luther and other Protestant state religions as well) took advantage of an ancient law known as the Justinian Law, which was a leftover from the old Roman Empire. This law allowed the infant baptism churches to label someone a "heretic" if they did not agree with their doctrine and turn them over to the state as a criminal and have them put in prison, tortured and often burned at the stake.

The Apostle Peter had given instructions for those who wished to be reconciled to God. They were told to repent, be baptized and receive the gift of the Holy Spirit—not only that, every one of them was to be baptized once they received Jesus as their Lord and Savior:

> And Peter answered them, Repent (change your views and purpose to accept the will of God in your inner selves instead of rejecting it) and be baptized, every one of you, in the name of Jesus Christ for the forgiveness of and release from your sins; and you shall receive the gift of the Holy Spirit.
>
> (Acts 2:38 AMP)

Prejudice against those who continued to be baptized in the above manner was escalating in this nation as well as in the old world. Violence against those who would not practice infant baptism was building in the new land, just like in the old Roman Empire. However, there was one difference—in the colonies, there was no law on the books whereby one denomination was allowed to have someone killed if they did not like their doctrine!

The growing prejudice against those who stayed true to New Testament teaching was building. Only one group of believers met with more hatred than the Baptists—this was the Quakers. Dolly Madison, who was to become one of America's first ladies, came from a Quaker family. Few know this for she did not fit even her mother's image of what a good, solid, serious Quaker girl should be. She loved gaiety too much and she loved pretty clothes and parties way too much.

There was a member of the Congregational church named James Madison, however, who did not disapprove of her at all. He was later to be president of the United States and he would need a good hostess to help carry out his duties. He was, in fact, fascinated with Dolly. He had never observed a Quaker up close before. He thought she was a typical Quaker, filled with charm and gaiety. Soon he was completely smitten with her; and she with him.[3]

Later he would marry the widow Dolly and they made a good team throughout their marriage and his political career, including president of the

---

[3] http://www.pbministries.org/History/John%20T.%20Christian/vol2/history2_part2_02.htm

United States. But God had additional purposes for the unusual-for-that-day marriage. Dolly's relatives were friends with an influential Baptist minister named Rev. John Leland.

Rev. Leland was a fiery preacher and emphatic that the United States needed a clause inserted in its new Constitution that protected freedom of religion. This was far-thinking in those days. So closely founded was our Constitution on Judeo-Christian principles that the need to protect religious freedom seemed inconceivable, even laughable.

But Rev. John Leland would not hear of it! He was aware of the murderous rampage of the Catholic church all across Europe and was concerned lest it happen in the new world, as well. Those who knew Rev. Leland were urging him to run as a delegate to the Virginia Convention on Ratification to make sure an amendment for freedom of conscience was added to the new Constitution. After much thought, he agreed to run.[4]

This conflicted with James Madison's aspirations to the same office. Madison already had a reputation as a champion of the underdog. He was well-respected in government circles but he did not have a forceful personality. It was thought that if Rev. Leland ran for the office, he would win handily because of his popularity.

Dolly's family saw the rivalry building and they

---

[4]pennstatelawreview.org/articles/113%20Penn%20St.%20L.%20Rev.%20733.pdf

arranged a meeting between the two men in a nearby park. There the rivals met to discuss their coinciding interests. They discovered they were on the same side of the issue but were being inspired by different motives. Madison wanted to be involved in politics; while Leland wanted the gospel free to go out unhindered.

As a result of their meeting and with a new respect and understanding for each other's objectives, Rev. Leland returned to preaching and James Madison, his election uncontested by Leland, entered the contest for delegate to the Virginia Convention and won.

In 1774 James Madison successfully maneuvered to put in place what Thomas Jefferson would later call "a wall of separation between church and state." Its purpose was to keep church denominations from attacking each other:

"Congress shall make no laws touching religion, or infringing the rights of conscience."

Madison's simple words were revised many times and finally ended up in the First Amendment to the United States Constitution where they passed into law and still stand today.[5]

> "Congress shall make no law respecting an establishment of religion, or prohibiting the free exercise thereof; or abridging the freedom of speech, or of the press; or the right of the people peaceably to assemble, and to petition the government for a redress of grievances."

---

[5] www.law.cornell.edu/wex/first_amendment

The Gospel of Jesus Christ was now free to go forth from the United States of America without being hindered by apostate churches.

The End

APPENDIX I

10 MYTHS OF INFANT BAPTISM

Myth 1: It is taught by some that babies are saved by infant baptism.

But the Bible does not say that. The following passage is almost always taken out of context. It is not about infant baptism. Jesus was responding to His disciples' question about which of them would be greatest in the kingdom of heaven.

> "Then Jesus called a little child to Him, set him in the midst of them, and said, "Assuredly, I say to you, unless you are converted and become as little children, you will by no means enter the kingdom of heaven. Therefore whoever humbles himself as this little child is the greatest in the kingdom of heaven."
>
> (Matthew 18:2–4)

Myth 2: It is taught by some that the following verse teaches a baptism of infants.

But the Bible does not say that. This verse is often taken out of context to refer to a baptism of infants even though there is no indication that Jesus sprinkled water on the children's heads. Jesus' method of laying-on of hands and praying was a typical Jewish blessing. Many denominations follow Jesus' example rather than infant baptism.

> "Then little children were brought to Him that He might put His hands on them and pray, but the disciples rebuked them. But Jesus said, "Let the little children come to Me, and do not forbid them; for of such is the kingdom of heaven." And He laid His hands on them and departed from there."
>
> (Matthew 19:13–15)

Myth 3: It is taught by some that infant baptism "saves" because Old Testament circumcision saved.

But the Bible says that Old Testament circumcision does not save. Nor did it ever. Therefore, if we are relying on the belief that infant baptism as a "thinly-veiled" *type* of circumcision "saves," we will fall from grace.

> "Indeed I, Paul, say to you that if you become circumcised, Christ will profit you nothing....you who attempt to be justified by law [ritual]; you have fallen from grace...For in Christ Jesus neither circumcision nor uncircumcision avails anything, but faith working through love."
>
> (Galatians 5:2, 4, 6)

> "For we say that faith was accounted to Abraham for righteousness. How then was it accounted? While he was circumcised, or uncircumcised? Not while circumcised, but while uncircumcised."
>
> (Romans 4:9–10)

Myth 4: It is taught by some that infant baptism is a type of Old Testament circumcision.

But the Bible does not say that. First, there

is no record of infant baptisms in the New Testament church. Second, the Bible does not say that Infant Baptism is a thinly veiled type of circumcision (or any other kind).

Myth 5: It is taught by some that infant baptism is scriptural because all households included infants.

But the Bible does not say that. There are five examples of household baptisms given in the New Testament. In four examples, it is clear that all first believed and then were baptized.

<blockquote>
The jailer's household (See Acts 16:16–34, esp. v. 34.)

Cornelius' household (See Acts 10:1–48, esp. vv. 1, 44.)

Stephanas' household (See 1 Corinthians 16:15.)

Crispus' household (See Acts 18:8.)
</blockquote>

In the fifth example, the Bible does not specifically state that Lydia's whole household believed before they were baptized. On the other hand, it infers that this is true. We know Lydia and her household were devout believers in God. We know that the apostle Paul expounded the gospel to all gathered at the river for their prayer time and that all responded to his preaching by being baptized, so they probably were believers. But, the Bible is silent on that point. Thus, infant baptism theology seems to rest on the silence of this verse, since the Bible clearly states that circumcision does not save and, in fact, causes one to fall from grace.

Myth 6: It is taught by some that infant baptism is necessary so that babies do not go into *Limbo* should they die prematurely.

But the Bible does not say that. It says that God considers the offspring of believers to be holy. This is the same word *holy*, as used in the Bible for the Holy Spirit. God would not send His Holy Spirit to hell, and believer's babies do not go into hell (Limbo).

> "For the unbelieving husband is sanctified by the wife, and the unbelieving wife is sanctified by the husband; otherwise your children would be *unclean*, but now they are *holy*."
> (1 Corinthians 7:14, Emphasis Added)

The infant baptism myth about babies dying and going into Limbo does not come from the Bible. It comes out of the mythology of heathenism. The reader of Greek and Roman classics will recognize Limbo from the Roman drama *The Aeneid*. Written by the well-known author Virgil, it tells of the plight of his character *Aeneas*.

The story tells of Aeneas's visit to the horrific sulfur and flame-filled regions of the netherworld. There Aeneas finds the souls of tormented babies who, having been torn from their mother's breasts in death, must remain in Limbo outside hell's gates without ever having hope of heaven because their parents had not made sure they were given the rites of baptism before they died.

> Before the gates the cries of babes new-born,
> whom fate had from their tender mothers torn,

assault his ears.[1]

In other words, out of ancient Roman mythology comes the belief that a baptism of babies is necessary so they don't die and go to hell (go into Limbo). For centuries, the Roman Catholic Church taught a belief in something called Limbo, but on December 5, 2006, the pope called a news conference to let the world know that they had changed their mind. Babies would not now be sent to Limbo if they died unbaptized.

Pope Benedict XVI said that, all along, Limbo had merely been a hypothesis of their church. Because they were getting so many calls from distraught grandparents and mothers about what happened to aborted babies, he said they decided to drop Limbo from Catholic beliefs.

Myth 7: It is taught by some theologians that infant baptism joins us to the family of God.

But the Bible doesn't say this. It says the Holy Spirit joins us to the family of God! Infant baptism is stealing credit for something done by God's Holy Spirit.

> "For by one Spirit, we were all baptized into one body—whether Jews or Greeks, whether slaves or free—and have all been made to drink into one Spirit."
>
> (1 Corinthians 12:13)

---

[1] Virgil, *The Aeneid, Book 6.ll,* 576–578, Dryden's Translation—Original, ll, 427–429.

Myth 8: It is taught by some that the Holy Spirit is given through infant baptism.

But the Bible does not say that. It says the Holy Spirit is given by faith in Jesus' finished work of the cross. The Bible says we cannot receive the Holy Spirit by a ritual, only by faith:

> "O foolish Galatians!...Did you receive the Spirit by the works of the law, or by the hearing of faith? Are you so foolish? Having begun in the Spirit, are you now being made perfect by the flesh?...For as many as are of the works of the law are under the curse; for it is written, "Cursed is everyone who does not continue in all things which are written in the book of the law, to do them." But that no one is justified by the law in the sight of God is evident, for "the just shall live by faith."
>
> (Galatians 3:1-3, 10-11)

Myth 9: It is taught by some that because John the Baptist sovereignly received the Holy Spirit while still in his mother's womb, that the Holy Spirit can be imparted by a minister during infant baptism.

But this is not true today. John the Baptist was of a different dispensation. During the Old Testament times, the Holy Spirit anointed for service (sovereignly came upon) prophets, kings, and priests for a specific task. John the Baptist's situation was that he was anointed to be a prophet while still in his mother's womb, and thus the Spirit of God was given to him at that time. The old covenant was in effect at that time because Jesus had not yet shed His

Blood, which ratified the new covenant. But under the new covenant, there are no examples given of the Holy Spirit empowering people before they are born.

Myth 10: It is taught by some that the Great Commission teaches that baptism saves.

The Bible does not teach this. It specifically states that salvation is by faith, for it says that if one does not believe, he will be condemned.

> "He who believes and is baptized will be saved; but he who does not believe will be condemned."
>
> (Mark 16:16)

It is important to note the word *saved* in this passage does not just mean "going to heaven." It means that and more, including deliverance and provision while here on earth.

When the above verse is read with this knowledge in mind, the verse fits neatly into New Testament doctrine.

> Saved (Greek, *sozo*): *Save* means the spiritual and eternal salvation granted to new believers immediately upon their conversion. Included in the word, saved, is temporal deliverance, material provision, deliverance from danger, etc., as well as eternal life.[2]

---

[2] *Hebrew-Greek Key Word Study Bible*, 1760.

Thus, a correct understanding of the Mark 16:16 verse which includes the word *saved*, would be as follows: "They who do not believe will be condemned; however, they who both believe and are baptized will receive future spiritual benefits because of their faith plus temporal benefits while down here on Earth when they become a Christian."

APPENDIX II

BACK TO FAITH ALONE

Jesus Christ, as our Redeemer, is coming soon. At that time, those who have placed their faith in Him but have not yet died and ascended to heaven will rise to meet Him in the air. In order to be accepted in this number, Jesus described an experience we must have. His terminology for it was "born again:"

> Jesus answered and said unto him: "Verily, verily, I say unto thee, "Except a man be born again, he cannot see the kingdom of God...Marvel not that I said unto thee, Ye must be born again."
>
> (John 3:3, 7 KJV)

> Jesus said to him, "I am the way, the truth, and the life. No one comes to the Father except through Me."
>
> (John 14:6)

> "All that the Father gives Me will come to Me, and the one who comes to Me I will by no means cast out."
>
> (John 6:37)

> "For all have sinned and fall short of the glory of God, being justified freely by His grace through the redemption that is in Christ Jesus, whom God set forth as a propitiation by His blood, though faith, to demonstrate His righteousness, because in His forbearance God had passed over the sins

that were previously committed, to demonstrate at the present time His righteousness, that He might be just and the justifier of the one who has faith in Jesus."

(Romans 3:23-26)

"If you confess with your mouth the Lord Jesus and believe in your heart that God has raised Him from the dead, you will be saved. For with the heart one believes unto righteousness, and with the mouth confession is made unto salvation. ...Whoever believes on Him will not be put to shame. ... For "whoever calls upon the name of the LORD shall be saved."

(Romans 10:9-11, 13)

God made it simple for us because He is not willing that any should perish.[1] If you want eternal life and believe that Jesus is God's Son and that He died, was buried, and resurrected, tell Him. Pray your own prayer, or say something like this:

God, I believe that Jesus is Your only begotten Son and that He died, was buried, and that He rose again. I choose to make Jesus the Lord of my life. Come into my heart, Lord Jesus. Amen.

Now, be baptized in water! Make Jesus truly Lord of your life. The Bible says,

"Or do you not know that as many of us as were baptized into Christ Jesus were baptized into His death? Therefore we were buried with Him

---

[1] 2 Peter 3:9

through baptism into death, that just as Christ was raised from the dead by the glory of the Father; even so we also should walk in newness of life. For if we have been united together in the likeness of His death, certainly we also shall be *in the likeness of His resurrection,"*

(Romans 6:3-5)

In other words, water baptism is important. IF we die with Christ, we will also *rise to newness of life*. It is an action we take to show our faith in Christ's finished work of the cross on our behalf. Just as Abraham the Old Testament patriarch of our faith submitted to the ritual of circumcision to show his faith was genuine (at the same time, giving his descendants a ritual whereby they could also be included in God's covenant), we submit to water baptism—as a *type of spiritual circumcision*. (See Col.2:11-12.)

Being baptized into the name of Jesus Christ for the remission of sin is not an optional action. You are commanded to *"repent, ... be baptized in the name of Jesus Christ for the remission of sins; and you shall receive the gift of the Holy Spirit."* (Acts 2:38) While it does not save us (Christ's shed blood has already provided salvation) the Bible is quite clear that there is an "IF" included. IF we are united with Christ in water baptism, we will also rise to newness of life, (Rom.6:4).

What if we were baptized as infants? We are to be rebaptized! If we have been baptized into something other than Jesus' name, we are to be rebaptized. Rebaptism is not a problem for God.

In the early Church, rebaptism was dealt with as a very unimportant issue as long as the new disciples received the Bible baptism of believers, that of the baptism into the name of Jesus. (See Acts 19:1-6.)

Then tell your priest or pastor that you want to take part in biblical water baptism. This is the after-conversion/full-immersion baptism as performed in the Book of Acts. The Bible says "let every one of you" take part in this baptism. It is for every believer. It is the way of the Cross.

God's provision for us was never to change until the second coming of Christ and includes receiving the gift of the Holy Spirit. In all the examples given in the Book of Acts after the Day of Pentecost,[2] if the Holy Spirit was not openly manifested, before or after water baptism, disciples were dispatched to lay hands on them and bring them into that experience. Neither water baptism nor receiving the Holy Spirit was taken casually.

If your pastor or priest won't baptize you (or rebaptize you) after you believe, God will help you find one that will, for this is the full program of God. Baptism doesn't save you, but it shows God that your faith is genuine.

> "Repent, and let every one of you be baptized in the name of Jesus Christ for the remission of sins; and you shall receive the gift of the Holy

---

[2] Samaritans—Acts 8:1, 17; Ethiopian eunuch—Acts 8:26–38; Saul/Paul's conversion—Acts 9:1–19; Cornelius's household—Acts 10:1–48; Lydia's household–Acts 16:11–15; Philippians jailer's household—Acts 16:25–34; the Ephesians—Acts 19:1–10

> Spirit. For the promise is to you and to your children, and to all who are afar off, as many as the Lord our God will call."
>
> (Acts 2:38-39)

Reflect and decide now. The Bible says that faith without actions is dead.[3] Jesus commanded baptism.[4] Be baptized in water *and the Spirit...!*

---

[3] James 2:17
[4] Matthew 28:19; Mark 16:16

AUTHOR'S PAGE

Judith McClary is a lifelong student of the Bible. She has an ecumenical understanding of various church doctrines because of her curiosity over why the "Church" is divided into two branches, has two different baptisms and teaches two wildly-different ways of salvation. Baptized into the Presbyterian church at six-weeks of age, McClary taught pre-teens, teens and adults, was board member of *Presbyterian Renewal,* leader of spiritual growth groups, writer of Bible study curriculum, pre-school department supervisor, T-V assistant and camera person and care minister. To contact the author or invite her to speak; e-mail or visit her website:

judymcclary@gmail.com
www.doesbaptismsave.com

AUTHOR'S BOOKS

1 DOES BAPTISM SAVE? – Must reading for those who believe their baptism saved them.

2 POPE FRANCIS SAYS COME HOME TO MOTHER - But to which mother? Jesus' mum? The mother of God? *Or is it the mother of the sun god?* Interesting reading.

3 GODDESSES IN THE CHURCH - THE INFANT BAPTISM CONNECTION: A second look at the 90's RE-imagining Conferences which introduced goddess worship & homosexuality to Protestant churches and the surprising discovery of the same issues in the Roman Catholic church.

4 SEVEN LETTERS TO THE INFANT BAPTISM CHURCH: *A LAYPERSON SPEAKS OUT* – A layperson's letters to her Lutheran church as she uncovers the false doctrine of infant baptism.

5 WATER BAPTISM & THE BLOOD COVENANT: New Testament believers are given a way to enter God's blood covenant. Have you been baptized *since you believed?*

6 I WENT TO BAPTIST KID'S CAMP & CAME HOME SPEAKING IN TONGUES: *A Holy Ghost Story* - An un-churched child receives the ancient Book of Acts experience when she attends Bible camp for the first time.

7 A DARK HORSE? THE MORMON CHURCH & THE ANTICHRIST – This book exposes a plagiarized Book of Mormon and how Joseph Smith, Jr. fooled his early followers using a "peep-stone" in his hat.

8 INFANT BAPTISM STALKS THE NEW TESTAMENT CHURCH – The Church has two different branches, two different water baptisms and teaches two wildly-different ways of gaining salvation—*find out how this has affected Church history.*

BIBLIOGRAPHY

Alex, Ben. *Martin Luther: The German Monk Who Changed the Church.* Victor Books/SP Publications, Inc., 1995.

Anderson, Sir Norman. *Christianity and World Religions.* Leicester, England: InterVarsity Press, 1984.

Arendzen, J. P. "Gnosticism," *New Advent: The Catholic Encyclopedia,* Vol. 6. New York, 1909. www.newadvent.org.

Armstrong, O. K. and Armstrong M. M. *The Indomitable Baptists.* Garden City, NJ: Doubleday & Company, 1967.

Beale, J. L. *Rise to Newness of Life.* Nappanee, IN: Evangel Press, 1974.

Bettenson, H. S., ed. *Documents of the Christian Church,* 2nd ed. London, England: Oxford University Press, 1963.

Bingham, D. Jeffrey. *Pocket History of the Church.* Downers Grove, IL: InterVarsity Press, 2002.

Booker, R. *The Miracle of the Scarlet Thread.* Shippensburg, PA: Destiny Image Publishers, 1981.

Brant, I. *James Madison: 1787-1800.* Indianapolis, IN: Bobbs-Merrill Company, 1950.

Broadbent, E. H. *The Pilgrim Church.* Grand Rapids, MI: Gospel Folio Press, 1999.

Brim, B. *The Blood and the Glory.* Tulsa, OK: Harrison House, 1995.

Bruce, F. F. *The International Bible Commentary with the NIV.* Grand Rapids, MI: Zondervan Publishing House, 1979.

Bruce. F. F. *The Spreading Flame.* Grand Rapids, MN: Wm. B. Erdmans Publishing, 1995.

The Catechism of the Catholic Church. Mahwah, NJ: Paulist Press, 1994.

Dake, Finis Jennings. *Dake's Annotated Reference Bible.* Lawrencevill, GA. Dake Publishing, Inc. 1999.

Davies, J. G. *The Early Christian Church.* New York: Holt, Rinehart, and Winston, 1965.

DeArteaga, W. *Quenching the Spirit: Examining Centuries of Opposition to the Movement of the Holy Spirit.* Lake Mary, FL: Creation House, 1992.

Dickens, A. G. *The Counter Reformation.* New York: Harcourt, Brace & World, 1969.

Dolan, J. P. *History of the Reformation.* New York: Descleo Company, 1965.

Dyck, C. J., ed. *An Introduction to Mennonite History.* Scottsdale, PA: Herald Press, 1967.

Erikson, E. H. *Young Man Luther: A Study in Psychoanalysis and History.* New York, NY: Norton, 1958.

Foxe, J. *Foxe's Books of Martyrs.* Springdale, PA: Whitaker House, 1981.

Foxe, John, rewritten and updated by Harold J. Chadwick, *Foxe's Book of Martyrs: Updated to the 21st Century.* Gainesville, FL: Bridge-Logos, 2001.

Friedenthal, R. *Luther: His Life and Times.* New York: Harcourt, Brace & Jovanovich, 1970.

Gollian, G. L. *Moravian in Two Worlds.* New York: Columbia University Press, 1967.

Grimm, H. J. *The Reformation Era: 1500-1650.* New York: Macmillan, 1973.

Gundry, R. H. *A Survey of the New Testament,* 3rd ed. Grand Rapids, MI: Zondervan Publishing House, 1994.

Hayford, J. *Hayford's Bible Handbook.* Nashville, TN: Thomas Nelson Publishers, 1995.

Hinn, B. *The Blood.* Orlando, FL: Creation House, 1993.

Hislop, A. *The Two Babylons.* Neptune, NJ: Loizeaux Brothers, 1916.

Horn, W. M. *Growth in Grace.* Philadelphia, PA: Muhlenberg Press, 1951.

Hostetler, J. A. *Hutterite Society.* Baltimore, MD: John Hopkins University Press, 1974.

Hostetler, J. & Huntington, G. *The Hutterites in North America.* New York: Holt, Rinehart, and Winston, 1980.

Huggins, L. *The Blood Speaks.* South Plainfield, NJ: Bridge Publications, 1954.

Hunt, D. *A Woman Rides the Beast.* Eugene, OR: Harvest House Publishers, 1994.

Hurstfield, J. *The Reformation Crisis.* New York: Barnes & Noble, 1965.

Inter-Lutheran Commission on Worship. *The Lutheran Book of Worship.* Minneapolis, MN: Augsburg Publishing House, 1978.

Jensen, I. L. *Jensen's Survey of the Old Testament.* Chicago, IL: Moody Press, 1978.

Kempis, T. *The Imitation of Christ.* London: Oxford University Press, 1920.

Kenyon, E. W. *The Blood Covenant, 28th ed.* Lynnwood, WA: Kenyon's Gospel Publishing Society, 1969.

BIBLIOGRAPHY

KJV-Amplified Holy Bible: Parallel Bible. Grand Rapids, MI: Zondervan Publishing House, 1995.

Leonard, E. G., Reid, J. M., trans. and ed. Rowley, H. H. *A History of Protestantism: The Reformation,. Vol. 1.* Indianapolis, IN: Bobbs-Merill, 1968.

Loewen, Harry and Nolt, Steven. *Through Fire & Water: An Overview of Mennonite History.* Scottsdale, PA: Herald Press, 1996.

Lohse, M. *Martin Luther: An Introduction to His Life and Work.* Philadelphia, PA: Fortress Press, 1986.

Luther, M. *Ninety-Five Theses: Address to the German Nobility Concerning Christian Liberty.* New York: Collier, 1965.

Manns, P. *Martin Luther: An Illustrated Biography.* New York: Crossroad, 1982.

McClary, J. M. *The Secret About Infant Baptism That Everyone's Missing.* (Lake Mary, FL. Creation House. 2008.)

Mjorud, H. *What's Baptism All About?* Carol Stream, IL: Creation House, 1978.

Murray, A. *The Power of the Blood of Jesus.* Springdale, PA: Whitaker House, 1993.Norris, R. A., Jr. *The Christological Controversy.* Philadelphia, PA: Fortress Press, 1980.

Oberman, H. *Luther: A Man Between God and the Devil.* New Haven, CT: Yale University Press, 1989.

O'Donnell, J. J. *Augustine.* Boston, MA: Twayne Publishers, 1985.

Office of the Presbyterian General Assembly. *The Work of the Holy Spirit.* Philadelphia, PA: United Presbyterian Church in the United States of America, 1978.

O'Neill, J. *Martin Luther.* New York: Cambridge University Press, 1975.

Oyer, J. S. and Kreider, R. S. *Mirror of the Martyrs.* Intercourse, PA: Good Books, 1990.

Prince, D. *Appointment in Jerusalem.* Grand Rapids, MI: Chosen Books, 1975.

Reimer, M. L., ed. *Christians Courageous.* Waterloo, Ontario: Mennonite Publishing Service, 1988.

Richardson, D. *Eternity in Their Hearts.* Ventura, CA: Regal Books, 1981.

Rives, Richard M. *Too Long in the Sun.* (Partakers Publications, Charlotte, NC. 1997.

Rost, S., ed. *Martin Luther: The Best From All His Works.* Nashville, TN: Thomas Nelson, 1989.

Sachar, Leon, Ph.D. *A History of the Jew,* 5th *ed.* New York: Alfred A. Knopf, 1967.

Simon, E. *Luther Alive: Martin Luther and the Making of the Reformation.* Garden City, NY: Doubleday, 1968.

Schmeman, Alexander. *The Historical Road of Eastern Orthodoxy.*

Smith, C. H. *Story of the Mennonites.* Newton, KS: Mennonite Publication Office, 1950.

Spitz, L. W. *The Protestant Reformation.* Englewood Cliffs, NJ: Prentice-Hall, 1966.

Strong, J. *The Strong's Exhaustive Concordance of the Bible.* Nashville, TN: Thomas Nelson Publishers, 1996.

Tenney, M. C. *New Testament Times.* Grand Rapids, MN: Wm B. Erdmans Publishing Company, 1978.

Todd, J. M. *Luther.* New York: Crossroad, 1982.

Trumbull, H. C. *The Blood Covenant: A Primitive Rite and Its Bearing on Scripture.* Kirkwood, MO: Impact Books, 1975.

van Braght, T. J. *Martyrs Mirror.* Scottsdale, PA: Herald Press, 1950.

Vine, W.E. *Vine's Expository Dictionary of Old & New Testament Words.* Nashville, TN. Thomas Nelson, Inc., 1997.

The Waldenses. Angwin, CA: LLT Productions.

White, Ellen G. *The Great Controversy.* Mt. View, CA: Pacific Press Publ. Assn., 1956.

Whyte, Rev. H. A. M. *The Power of the Blood.* Springdale, PA: Whitaker House, 1973.

"Worshipping Like Pagans?" *Christian History,* Issue 37.

Yandian, B. *Galatians: The Spirit-Controlled Life.* Tulsa, OK: Pillar Book & Publishing Company, 1993.

www.ingramcontent.com/pod-product-compliance
Lightning Source LLC
Chambersburg PA
CBHW061430040426
42450CB00007B/989